The Shame Game

Leaving Shame to Live in Abundance

Janice Sterling Gaunt, LPC

Brown Books Publishing Group
Dallas, Texas

The Shame Game
Leaving Shame to Live in Abundance

The details and identifying circumstances in the case studies used in this book have been altered in order to protect the confidentiality of the author's clients. No one case study is representative of any individual, living or dead.

Brown Books Publishing Group
16200 North Dallas Parkway, Suite 170
Dallas, Texas 75248
brownbooks.com
(972) 381-0009

A New Era in Publishing.™

ISBN 978-1-934812-92-1
Library of Congress Control Number 2011921830

Printed in the United States of America
10 9 8 7 6 5 4 3 2 1

Author photo by Rusty Bradford Photography

For more information about Janice or *The Shame Game*, please visit janicegaunt.com.

I lovingly dedicate this book to my amazing and oh-so-precious daughters, Brynn, Wesley, and Blair. Simply being in your presence makes my heart dance and my soul sing.

Contents

Part 4
DOING THE WORK: MENTAL BOOT CAMP

Part 5
LIVING IN ABUNDANCE: YOU ABSOLUTELY DESERVE IT

Foreword

Why do some people naturally seem to possess a buoyancy, a clear sense of self, and confidence, while others seem to eat themselves alive, turning against themselves along a spectrum of violence ranging from the merely neurotic to the virulence of an autoimmune disorder? The confident person possesses healthy self-esteem. While the person suffering from self-attack is swamped by unhealthy shame.

As described by Pia Mellody, a mentor to both Janice and me, healthy self-esteem and healthy shame are synonyms, two phrases for the same capacity: the ability to hold ourselves in warm regard despite our imperfections. There are two elements to this description. First, there is the ability to hold oneself warmly. Second, there is the recognition of our limitations and flaws. It is that recognition that is the job of healthy shame.

Healthy shame is a gift that keeps us human; it keeps our feet on the ground and renders us humble, accountable, and good. Unhealthy shame, also known as toxic shame, eats away at our souls like a cancer. Unhealthy shame has the power to impair your sense of well-being and worth, lead to addictions, destroy relationships, and even cost you your life. What a powerful thing shame is. Too little of it—being shameless—is grotesque. Too much, or more precisely the wrong *kind* of shame, can ruin you. What is the difference between the two and how do we get from the enormous destructiveness of the unhealthy version to the blessings of the healthy one? Where do either or both versions come from? These are some of the questions tackled in *The Shame Game*.

Generally most of us will relate to ourselves the way we were related to in our childhoods. If we were held with kindness and respect, we hold ourselves that way. Such individuals are the lucky ones, those relative few who made it through their childhoods universally cherished and cared for—they are the possessors of healthy self-esteem in adulthood. Then there are the rest of us. If you were held critically by a parent or significant caregiver, the odds are that you will be critical of yourself. If held indulgently, you will indulge yourself. Any interaction between parent and child that is not nurturing is injurious, and those injuries show up in our most important relationship: the one we have with ourselves. In other words, trauma in childhood sets up self-esteem issues in adulthood.

What kind of trauma leads to which kind of self-esteem issues? One of Pia Mellody's most powerful insights is that there is not one singular type of psychological trauma in childhood; there are two. The one most of us think of most readily she calls "disempowering abuse," which means treating a child in ways that leave him or her feeling small or defective. These kinds of shaming behaviors can be as overt as hitting the child or telling them that they are bad, or it can be as subtle as turning to a martini at the end of the day and ignoring the child. When parents treat children in ways that convey the message that the child is worthless, the child invariably takes that message deep into their psyche, feeling as worthless as the message conveyed about them. This is inescapable. It's like physical law: go out in the rain without an umbrella or a raincoat, and you'll get soaked. I tell my clients, "Show me the thumbprint, and I'll tell you about the thumb." That is, show me an adult who has unhealthy shame, and I'll tell you about a childhood in which they were obviously or covertly shamed.

The second type of abuse, which Mellody calls "false empowerment," involves either deliberately pumping up the child's sense of entitlement or, not doing the parental job of setting appropriate limits and offering emotional education. Disempowering behaviors lead to issues of unhealthy shame—feeling worthless, bad, ugly, or stupid; behaviors that falsely empower lead to issues of grandiosity—feeling better than others, looking down your nose at someone or some group, or feeling above the rules. Neither of these states represents healthy self-esteem, and neither lets you fully love others. This is the psychological truth behind the old cliché that you can't love someone else unless you love yourself. Another way of saying this is that you can't be truly intimate with someone from a position of either inferiority or superiority. True love demands equality. Unhealthy self-esteem in either direction—shame or grandiosity—doesn't just create problems between you and you but between you and others as well.

Psychiatrist George Valiant once claimed that there were two kinds of people in the world: the guy who walks into an elevator, gets claustrophobic, and turns green, and the guy who lights up a big, fat stogie and makes everyone else turn green. That's the difference between shame and grandiosity. I would add that neither of the men in the story had much bandwidth for noticing the people with them. Neither enjoyed the ride. As Janice explains, the cure for both grandiosity and unhealthy shame is *healthy* shame—the ability to hold yourself warmly despite your human frailties or bad behavior. The trick is to feel appropriately bad about whatever you may have done while still feeling OK about who you are fundamentally, to hold yourself accountably and lovingly at the same time. For those of us who grew up in consistently healthy environments, we learned to hold ourselves this way from having been held that way by our parents and others. For those with more difficult upbringings, we must learn— sometimes painstakingly—how to strike this balance. Not experiencing it in our families, we learn it from books, watching others, and most of all, in an educational, healing environment like coaching or therapy. We learn to reparent ourselves with the help of a guide.

With her decades of experience as a therapist and in the recovery community, Janice proves an excellent and generous guide. She is generous in two ways: First, she is generous of mind, offering a thoroughgoing treatment of the subject, giving her readers a detailed map of the terrain and practical tools to reach their goal. Second, she is generous of heart, sharing her own story of injury and recovery. Janice's voice throughout the book is like that of a trusted friend, someone in the trenches with you, someone who has been there. She speaks with practical wisdom and clinical wisdom, but most of all, she speaks with the wisdom gained through her own difficult and miraculous journey, showing her struggles while always holding herself and her readers in warm, dignified regard. In doing so, throughout the book she models the very principles she espouses—as all good teachers should.

Her message is clear and one that I fully endorse: if shame drags you down, or if it's dragging down someone you love, do something about it. You can free yourself from the constraints and pain of unhealthy shame. Get to know your shame, its causes, its feel. Then use techniques like those in this book or those learned in therapy to form a new, more loving relationship with yourself and with others. Speaking as a therapist and teacher of over thirty years' experience, I will say to you, dear reader, what I say to my clients: I, too, have lived under the tyranny of unhealthy shame, and through a lot of hard work and effective support, I can say that I have broken through, and I live now in the democratic rule of health.

Health is better.

—Terrence Real
Author of *I Don't Want to Talk About It*,
How Can I Get Through to You?,
The New Rules of Marriage, and *Wonderful Marriage*

Author's Note

About six years ago the idea of writing a book began to roll around in my head. I wanted to be able to hand my clients a book that encapsulated what I believe about shame and how an individual could begin the process of healing and live a life filled with abundance. I thought that reading such a book could save my clients some time and money—they could literally take the information home and process it at their own pace.

Although there have been books that individually address shame, healing from that shame, and abundant living, I could not find a single book that brought together these three related issues. Most of my clients had no desire to read multiple self-help books, and the thought of reading a really long one made their eyes glaze over.

The book needed to be informative, understandable, and, most importantly, concise. Because I did not perceive myself as a "good writer" (I am sure there is some shame in that statement), I had no idea how to begin such an undertaking. As the result of encouragement from a friend who agreed to help me get started, my literary journey began.

Initially it was challenging for me to say what I wanted to say in just the right way. After working on the book for about six months, I had to put the material aside. It was just not right, and I could not figure out where I was missing the boat.

One morning around three, I awoke and literally sat up in bed. I realized that I was trying too hard to sound intelligent instead of simply being real and vulnerable. My old shame messages were rearing their heads, saying, "Janice, you need the reader to think that you are smart so that your value is established." I was actually doing what I was writing about not doing! Go figure.

I revamped the entire manuscript in the hope that the reader would be able to feel my deep warmth and compassion as he began his own self-exploration. I sincerely hope that I have accomplished that goal.

In 1995, I began one of the most painful journeys of my life. I realized that I was headed for divorce after twenty-two years of marriage. At the time of my divorce, I could not even say the "*D* word" without feeling great despair and sadness. I believed that I was an absolute failure, and I was terribly fearful that my three precious daughters would be eternally messed up. I remember sobbing uncontrollably in the fetal position on my closet floor as my three daughters stood by and helplessly watched.

Because I had no sense of self away from my marriage, I did not think that I would survive. Life as I knew it was ending and I literally wanted to die.

Fortunately I sought professional help and was able to begin again. My therapists educated me about shame and guided me down the path to healing. Because shame had greatly affected my ability to make sound life decisions, they taught me that I had to fix "my picker" so that I did not repeat the same experience in some alternate form.

As I began to heal my shame, they taught me to believe that I deserved abundance in all areas of my life. After I went through the process myself, I decided that if I could use my pain to help others with their pain, then the pain was not wasted but was actually purposeful.

This revelation inspired me to attend graduate school, and after four years of hard work and perseverance, I earned my master's degree in counseling and became a licensed professional counselor. I now know that I am doing exactly what I am supposed to be doing and that all of those experiences were necessary so that I could heal and in some small way contribute to the healing of others.

It is crucial that you read this book with an open heart and mind so that you can recognize where you have been and how your past has affected your present. I know that as you read *The Shame Game* you might be thinking (as I thought), *I am an adult now. . . . I should let the past go. . . . I know my parents did the best they could. . . . So many people had it worse than me. . . .* and so on. There is so much more to healing than that.

This is a book about *you* healing, not about your parents. I want you to start reading this book with no strings attached. There is no test. There is no pressure. You cannot do this wrong. This book is about changing *your* life so that you can experience the joy that awaits you.

Although there are many spiritual references throughout the book, this is not a denominational book. I use the terms "God," "the Universe," and "Higher Power" synonymously in reference to an all-loving divine entity. I use these references to help you connect to your *own* spirituality, whatever that may be. It may be a religion, nature, love, spirit, or simply your own undefined higher power. If you have trouble with this concept, please do not be discouraged or disillusioned—your own truth will be revealed to you.

It is an honor and a privilege to have you as a reader. If any part of *The Shame Game* inspires you or gives you hope for a better way of life, then once again, my pain was my gift.

Acknowledgments

Without great mentors, it would have been impossible for me to write this book and to do what I do with my clients. In 1999 I attended a Post Induction training workshop at The Meadows Treatment Center in Wickenburg, Arizona. It was there that Pia Mellody first introduced me to the concept of toxic shame. Pia taught me how the lack of nurturing love creates a wound within a child that affects the child throughout his life, and the importance of healing those childhood wounds. My training with Terrence Real, founder of the Relational Life Institute in Boston, Massachusetts, brought me into an even deeper understanding of toxic shame and grandiosity. Terry trained me to recognize the effects of toxic shame in relationships and to guide my clients on a path of relationship repair. Thank you, Pia and Terry, for your genius, your inspirational work, and for your generosity in sharing with me your wisdom and truth.

I would never have begun this incredible endeavor without the encouragement and organizational skills of Jason Hopcus. Thank you, Jason, for lighting the fire to get me started.

Natalie Dickinson, you are incredibly talented! I know without a shadow of a doubt that the Universe selected you to be my editor. Your loving spirit, abounding creativity, and attention to detail made the editing process a delight.

Thank you, Milli Brown and everyone at Brown Books, for believing in me and providing the resources to implement my vision.

To all of the women, men, and adolescents with whom I have worked, thank you! I greatly admire your courage and willingness to change. As your teacher, I have been your student.

Thank you, Tom, for believing in this project from the beginning. As a loving husband and friend, I cannot imagine anyone being more supportive. I also want to thank my mom, Josie Sterling, for encouraging my independence. To my daughters, Brynn Isom, Wesley Laughton, and Blair Isom, thank you for forgiving my "mothering blunders" and for cheering me along in my desire to participate in the healing of the world!

Introduction

*T*he *Shame Game* is a book about shame and the ways in which shame may be impeding your ability to live life abundantly. My intention is to define and explain toxic shame and introduce the healing process that is necessary for abundant living. I believe that abundant living is everyone's birthright, and the purpose of this book is to give you the tools to claim this inheritance.

The Shame Game is not intended to be comprehensive on these subjects. Rather my intention is that it will create within you a feeling of hope and excitement about changing your life experience.

If you are a parent, *The Shame Game* may trigger feelings of guilt and shame about the way that you have parented your children. Although this is a normal response to learning about the consequences of shameful parenting techniques, it is extremely important that you focus on *yourself* as a child rather than on your own children. After you reflect on your childhood experiences, become empathetically connected to your inner child, and gain an understanding of your inherent worth, you will then begin to accept yourself as an imperfect parent. You will be able to change your parenting practices and/or make amends to your children without feeling overwhelmed with guilt or shame.

I am a fellow traveler with you on this journey. I have done the healing work, felt the sadness and compassion for myself as a wounded child, and am practicing a life of rebuking shame so that I can claim the abundance that is here for all of us. Congratulations on having the courage to change.

A child is born. As you look at the child, your heart quickens and you become overwhelmed by the child's preciousness. Your senses come to attention as you grasp the miracle of birth. You marvel at the wonder of his body and the tender softness of his skin. As he finds his voice, the child insists on attention and care. Once you meet his demands, the child settles into a deep slumber as he nuzzles into the warmth of your arms. Your heart is filled with love.

But there is something more, something deeper. If you look into the child's eyes and even beyond his eyes into the depth of his soul, into his heart, you will recognize it. You will experience it. You have transcended from a belief into a knowing. You have entered into a very spiritual place. A place where you recognize the child's created value that was established as his birthright. The child's value exists simply because he exists.

You are now seeing the child through the eyes of the heart. You are seeing the child through the eyes of God. You now know with absolute certainty that this child, every child, is a child of the Creator. This child can never be of lesser value and has no need to obtain greater value. This child's value, his full preciousness, simply *is*.

This child is *you*. May you come to know it!

I

Introducing Toxic Shame:

One

"*All glory comes from daring to begin.*"
—Eugene F. Ware—

As a sophomore at Southern Methodist University, everyone expected Claire to be on cloud nine. In her freshman year, she had pledged a well-known sorority, earned an A average, frequently went out with friends, and was stunning in her appearance. Everyone thought that Claire had it all.

On a cool October morning, Claire's mother called me in a panic, desperately wanting to schedule an appointment for her daughter. "Claire told me that she wants to drop out of college," sobbed Claire's mother. "She is absolutely miserable and has been skipping classes. I can't imagine what could possibly be wrong with her. Some days Claire doesn't even get out of bed. I just can't take it. I am so worried about her."

Claire entered my office two days later and initially appeared to be a typical twenty-year-old woman. She was well groomed and polite and smiled warmly. When I asked Claire how I could help her, however, tears started streaming down *her face. "I absolutely hate my life," she said. "In the morning when my alarm rings, I just turn it off and go back to sleep. I can't get the energy to go to class or do my assignments. At night all I want to do is go out partying and try to find a guy to hook up with. I know I shouldn't be doing all of this, but it is the only way I can survive. I really hate myself!"*

I asked Claire if she had undergone a physical recently. She said that she had gone to see a doctor two months earlier and had gotten a clean bill of health. After eliminating the possibility of a physical illness, I asked, "Claire, do you like attending SMU?"

Claire's gaze dropped as she sat in silence for a couple of moments. "Actually, I had originally wanted to attend The University of Texas," answered Claire. "After applying and being accepted to UT, my father told me that he really wanted me to attend SMU. When I told him that I thought UT would be more fun for me, my father pouted for several days. I must have really hurt his feelings because he wouldn't even talk to me," said Claire.

I later learned that Claire's father had been a football star at SMU and had served on many SMU boards for years. He loved SMU and simply could not understand why Claire did not want to follow in his footsteps.

I also found out that Claire had wanted to pledge a different sorority than the one she did pledge. Claire had been pressured to pledge her mother's sorority in order to fulfill her mother's dream that Claire continue the legacy that had been in the family for generations. Claire thought that it was her duty to do what her mother desired for fear of disappointing her. After experiencing her father's dissatisfaction, Claire simply could not do the same thing to her mother.

Throughout our conversation, I realized that Claire had made many decisions throughout her life based on the desires of her parents. Rather than living her own life and being encouraged to embrace her own desires, Claire had spent twenty years living her parents' dreams. She had no sense of her own value and had not been given permission to be true to herself. In the process, Claire had become depressed and had lost herself in her relationships with boys. Spiraling downward and spinning out of control, Claire's life was not working. She was living her life from a place of shame.

One

Shame Versus Self-Esteem:

Stealing Candy from Your Inner Baby

Hello, My Name Is . . . Shame

You know the term. You definitely know the feeling. There s a great possibility, however, that you do not fully understand the meaning and power of shame. The majority of people do not. Even though you may have heard your parents or teachers say to you as a child, "Shame on you!" or "You should be ashamed of yourself!" you were probably unaware of the vast power of those words. All you knew was that it felt awful to be shamed. You walked away from the experience with your head down, shoulders slumped, and tears welling in your eyes. So what exactly is shame and how could it feel so humiliating?

---

*Shame is an emotion that tells you that your
inner self is not OK.*

Shame is an emotion that tells you that your inner self is not OK. It tells you that you are unworthy, dishonorable, and disgraceful. Because shame tends to gnaw and fester in your gut, it will not only make you uncomfortable but will also greatly damage your ability to see yourself as you really are. It creates in you the perception that something is fundamentally wrong within your very being. Although you may act as if you have everything together and the world may perceive you as such, your internal voice whispers, "It is a lie. You are not enough."

As you continue to demean yourself, the shame will grow and become excessive. In its pervasiveness, it will create a deep, gut-wrenching feeling that you are worthless, grossly inadequate, less than, and intrinsically bad. You will start to believe that your very existence is a mistake.

Not only is excessive shame uncomfortable, it is within itself toxic and can often become debilitating. As you buy into the message that you are inherently bad, the toxic shame starts to cloud or mask your ability to recognize your true inherent value. You become deluded into believing that your value has been lost or, at best, severely damaged. Picture a diamond that has been covered in mud. Although the diamond's value has not been altered in any way, the mud makes it impossible to recognize the intrinsic value of the diamond. Toxic shame is the mud that impairs your ability to know your inherent value.

Toxic shame will sabotage your ability to live life with spontaneity, joy, and authenticity, thus depleting you of vitality and energy. In order to compensate for the belief that your essence is not enough, you will subconsciously determine that you must act as if you are someone else.

You will take on the values and behaviors of those whom you perceive as being adequate so that you are acceptable in the eyes of others. If you are acceptable to others, you can then accept yourself. Because it is uncomfortable being in your own skin, you will develop the ability to become a chameleon depending upon the circumstances. Like a kite blowing in the wind, you will flail this way and that, depending upon the thinking and feeling reality of others. The continuation of this internal desperate process is absolutely exhausting.

In response to feeling ashamed, less than, or inferior, you will either stay in a place of inferiority or develop defense mechanisms that will delude you into believing that you are superior to others. Judgment, criticism, aggressiveness, and self-righteous indignation are some of the ways you may try to cover up your feelings of unworthiness or shame. Saying to yourself, "I am better than others," will temporarily ease the misery of shame. However, the relief will not last and the cover-up behaviors will continue.

In contrast, the absence of shame—or recognizing your true value—creates a feeling of humility. Life becomes a joyful experience as you live from a place of legitimacy and truth, free to be yourself.

Somewhere around four months of age, my first grandchild, Owen, started smiling—*really* smiling! When he smiled, every speck of his body radiated joy. His eyes would crinkle, his arms and legs would flail, and his fingers and toes would curl simultaneously. Of course, his joy was contagious as it was literally impossible for me or anyone else to not answer his smiles with smiles of our own. One day as I relished watching Owen in the deliciousness of his joy, it dawned on me: this is how we were all created. We were created to exude an almost irrepressible, spontaneous joy for simply living as who we are, a pure and untainted joy that affords us the freedom to play. So what happened to inhibit your capacity for this sort of boundless joy? Your thoughts were contaminated by the shame messages and the defeatism of others.

Humility also enables you to see yourself in true relation to others. You understand that you are not better than any other human being. Humility facilitates your ability to embrace your humanity, keeping you mindful of your need for a power greater than yourself. Both the awareness of your connection to a Higher Power and the awareness of your connection to mankind is in itself a spiritual experience.

While shame is about your inner self and your perception of your value, guilt is about your outer self—your words and actions.

As you begin to understand shame and recognize its presence in your life, it is important for you to be able to differentiate between guilt and shame. While shame is about your inner self and your perception of your value, guilt is about your outer self—your words and actions. Guilt is a valuable emotion because it is a warning sign that you may have acted outside of your value system. When you feel guilty about something, stop and ask yourself if you have said or done anything that is abusive or contrary to your values. If the answer is yes, make an apology, change your behavior, and then leave it alone. If you continue to feel guilty, you are probably feeling shame rather than guilt.

Remember to separate your actions from your value. It is valuable when identifying offenses to others that you know you are not responsible *for* the feelings and actions of other people. You are responsible *to* other people—to be honest and to be kind. Being honest means not lying and being kind means not being abusive. (Saying "No" is not unkind. Saying "No, you jerk" is unkind.)

Introducing . . . Self-Esteem

Like shame, people often talk about self-esteem without having a clue as to its real meaning. People will say that someone has either a lot of self-esteem or very little self-esteem. I cannot begin to tell you how often a parent will bring a troublesome adolescent into my office and say something like, "I think the problem is that my child has no self-esteem. If you will just get him to make better grades or realize how great he is at football (or some other activity), then he will have self-esteem."

In reality, self-esteem has nothing to do with accomplishments, beauty, or talent. Self-esteem is different from self-confidence in that self-confidence comes from realizing and believing that you have a particular talent, ability, or unique physical, emotional, or intellectual quality. Self-esteem, on the other hand, is simply knowing with absolute certainty that you are inherently valuable. As you see and love yourself as you truly are, you will experience self-respect, self-interest, and a sense of self-love. In essence, self-esteem is the opposite of shame.

When you were born, your value was established. This is true for everyone. That means that there are no bad people. There are people who behave in ways that are hurtful to others, but their behavior is separate from their birth-established value. If you were to stand at the window of a hospital nursery, it would be impossible to pick out the "bad" or "worthless" babies. That is because there is no such thing. Every child is created precious and worthy. It is important to recognize this truth so that you can truly believe in your own birth-created value.

If you believe that there is any chance whatsoever that any human being can be created less valuable than any other human being, you will subconsciously hold on to the possibility that you just might be the one who was created with less value. This possibility will reside deep within your spirit and will impede your ability to believe in the divine value of human beings. Consequently and most importantly, it will sabotage *your* ability to embrace the essence of *your own* value, thus diminishing your self-esteem.

What is interesting about your perception of being "less than" is that it is merely an illusion. You have been conditioned into believing a lie. The reality is that your preestablished value can *never* be less and has no need to be more. Your value is whole, complete, and static.

Your parents or primary caregivers played an essential role in rooting your concept of self-value or self-esteem. A parent's role is to nurture a child with care, love, and limit-setting so that the child's value is sustained and recognizable to the child. The result is that the child feels safe. Such caregiving, or nurturing, validates the child's esteem on a very basic level. This functional parenting process confirms the preciousness that already exists within the child.

Additionally your parent's own self-esteem further developed and sustained your value tank. A parent who comes to know his own preciousness in the eyes of God will then be able to transfer this knowing to the child. As the child gets older, his self-esteem will thrive and come into the child's awareness. The child begins to understand that he too is precious.

Chapter One Exercises:
What You Can Do

- Begin to recognize your own shame by noticing how you feel. If you feel like you are shrinking, stop and say to yourself, "I matter. I am valuable." If you are in a place where you can say this out loud, all the better! You will feel the shrinking in your gut and it will not feel pleasant. Repeat this exercise often and you will get in the habit of pulling yourself up from the shrinking feeling.
- Write "I am valuable!" on sticky notes and place them where you will see them often. Put them on your refrigerator, your bathroom mirror, your computer, and in your car. You cannot have too many of these notes. If friends or family members giggle about your notes, just smile and say, "Yes, I *do* matter and so do you!"

Two

"But words are more powerful than perhaps anyone suspects, and, once deeply engraved in a child's mind, they are not easily eradicated."

—May Sartone—

I vividly remember meeting Kevin for the first time. As he entered my office, I was immediately struck by his meticulous appearance and warm smile. Although Kevin had achieved wide recognition due to the success of his advertising company, I could see in his eyes that he was extremely sad.

"My life is a mess," he said. "I am really good at what I do in my business, but I simply cannot succeed in a relationship. The last guy I dated appeared to be 'the one,' but after nine months, I found out he was cheating on me. I desperately tried to make it work, thinking that I should be more attentive, work less, or be more understanding, but after three more months, he cheated on me again. . . . I guess I had a feeling from the start that this guy was a player. I mean, several people warned me of his past, but I kept thinking that if I only loved him in the right way he would be different with me. This is not the first guy who has done this; it's happened twice before. What is wrong with me? Why can't I seem to get it right?"

"You know, Kevin," I answered. "Sometimes we just keep doing the same thing over and over again expecting different results. I would really like to hear about your childhood and family. I am guessing that your past has had a fairly profound influence on your present."

Kevin wiped a lone tear from his cheek as he began talking about his youth. "I was raised in a small town in the Midwest," he said. "My family was a 'God-fearing' family that was an integral part of our small church community. My father was a church deacon and my mother taught Sunday school and sang in the choir. They were pillars of our town."

"What do you remember about attending that church? Was it fun for you?" I asked.

"Not really," answered Kevin. "I remember thinking that God expected me to be perfect. I was told that God would not tolerate any sort of evil behavior. It was scary to me, so I always tried to act in a way that would please God. When I was thirteen, I realized that I was attracted to other males. It really freaked me out. I tried to squelch my feelings because I thought about how devastated and embarrassed my parents would be. I also thought that God would be extremely displeased and would punish me in some horrible way. I tried dating girls, thinking that my attraction to males was just the work of the devil. Of course, it did not work and at age seventeen, I became depressed."

"That must have been really painful for you," I said. "When did you tell your parents that you were gay?"

"Well actually, the father of a friend of mine told my parents," replied Kevin. "At the end of my senior year, I finally got the courage to share my secret with my best friend. My friend was appalled and told me that I was going to go *to hell when I died. He told his father, who immediately told my father as well as the entire community. My father would not speak to me and my mother cried for days. It was terrible. Basically I was banned from the church and became the laughingstock of the town. I was ostracized from all of my friends and teased mercilessly. The day after I graduated from high school, I left that town and did not return until after I graduated from college."*

"Kevin, I am so sorry that you had to experience that as a young man," I said. "You were given the message from a lot of people that who you were was not OK, not only from their perspective but also in the eyes of God. Those toxic shame messages have played themselves out in your relationships with others as well as in your relationship with yourself. You have been a victim of the shame game."

Two

Shame-Based Influences:

The Faces of Shame

Nurturing love sustains the birth-given value of a child and greatly enhances a child's ability to flourish.

A s I have already stated, an essential component in the rooting of self-esteem is nurturing love. Nurturing love sustains the birth-given value of a child and greatly enhances a child's ability to flourish. If your parents received nurturing love from their parents, they would have realized their own intrinsic value, thus enabling them to parent you with nurturing love. Parents with self-esteem are able to express nurturing love with very little difficulty.

"So what is nurturing love?" you may ask. Basically nurturing love is parenting a child for the sole purpose of filling the child with an unshakable awareness of his own inherent worth. It is that simple. In order for a parent to accomplish this important goal, the parenting process needs to include the following:

- The ability to set limits for the child without the withdrawal of physical or emotional affection
- Meeting the child's physical needs
- Physical and emotional presence of the caregiver
- Not using the child to meet the parent's emotional or physical needs
- A parent's acknowledgement of their own imperfections and an ability to allow the child to embrace their own humanness
- Absence of verbal, physical, intellectual, spiritual, or sexual abuse
- Congruency between words and behavior
- The experience and expression of joy within the family

When a child/emerging adult experiences a lack of nurturing love, self-value is masked, shame begins to emerge, and a shame core develops. This process happens through exposure to external influences where shame-based messages are taught.

Parental Shame

Without a doubt, your parents or other primary caregivers had the most significant influence on the way you learned to view your value. From the moment of your birth, you looked to your parents for sustenance, acceptance, and approval. Your parents were the barometers that revealed your value to you.

It is noteworthy to stress that both parents need to avoid shaming a child. If one of the parents sends a child shame-based messages and the other parent sits silently watching, the silent parent is in essence confirming the shameful message. There are many possible ways that parents can shame a child; these are discussed in the next chapter.

School Shame

Teachers and school administrators also have a powerful influence on a child's perception of self. School authority figures often label children by using shameful messages such as:

- Good versus bad
- Smart versus stupid
- Successful versus a failure

Many times children are only acknowledged when they are high achievers. This sets us up for performance esteem and perfectionism. It can establish in a child's mind that they are less valuable if they do not measure up to the criteria established by the schools.

Our school systems, for the most part, place more emphasis on high achievement in an academic classroom than artistic endeavors such as art, music, drama, and craftsmanship. In this sort of environment, a child who is more right-brained is considered less valuable than a child who is more left-brained. If you had any sort of learning difference, then you probably got a double whammy— not only did you perform below perfection, but you also needed extra help to learn a concept or additional time to complete a task.

Another factor to consider is that a child in a highly academic school may regard anything less than an A as being bad. Making one or more Cs, which is still a passing grade, is regarded by many schools and parents as inadequate.

If you were expected to make all As, then I am sure you felt a lot of pressure. This sort of pressure creates a shaming, stress-filled academic experience instead of an esteeming, pleasurable learning experience.

It is also very important that teachers are careful about the emotional abuse of children in regard to humiliating and embarrassing children in front of their peers. I know of a third-grade teacher who used the shortest girl and tallest boy in her class as examples of the meaning of short and tall. She told the two children to stand in front of the class as she talked about the difference in their size. The children felt embarrassed as their classmates giggled. Even as an adult, the student who was used to represent short still remembers that experience as being emotionally painful and shaming.

Another example is that of a fourth-grade teacher who put up a bulletin board in his classroom stating that one of the students (the teacher actually used the student's name) was the world's biggest procrastinator. I saw this student as a client when she was in college. One of her difficulties was procrastination; it was greatly affecting her ability to complete her degree. The young adult had literally fulfilled the prophecy that the teacher had so insensitively created.

Both situations were horribly shameful. The children were used in ways that were demeaning and humiliating.

There is absolutely no place in a classroom for the shaming of children. If parents are aware of this type of behavior, they should absolutely intervene.

Religious Shame

Religious leaders, Sunday school teachers, and parents intensely influence a child's perception of self. When this is done in negative ways, it produces deep shame. Some examples of negative religious influences are:

- Fanaticism
- Rigidity
- The concept of being born unworthy
- Conditional acceptance and love from God
- Spiritual superiority

Religious shame is horrifically damaging to a child/emerging adult's self-esteem. It can be one of the most destructive and difficult to heal of all the shaming messages. It erodes an individual at the very core of his being. If one perceives that he is unworthy in the eyes of his Higher Power, then he will continually view himself as being inadequate. In his perception, he was doomed at the moment of his birth and can never sufficiently right the wrong.

A spiritually superior person is one who believes that their religious beliefs are the only way. Their viewpoint excludes anyone else's right to think differently and creates an individual who is spiritually "one up" and superior. If you were taught that your church possessed the only true belief system that is honored by God, you will tend to assert that those who believe differently are condemned. This could create a sense of spiritual insecurity as you may have tried to reconcile how an all-loving Higher Being can doom any of His children to eternal exile. Both as a child and as an adult you believe "If it can happen to another, it can certainly happen to me."

You must truly believe that your Higher Power looks at you and thinks, "You rock just because you exist!"

If you experienced religious shame as a child, you may have a very difficult time developing a healthy concept of a Higher Power or God. Because I believe that self-esteem and a belief in an all-loving Higher Power go hand in hand, it is important to clear away your childhood concept of God and start over. You will need to create an image of a Higher Power or God who does not judge, punish, or send difficulties to you or anyone else. You will have to learn to trust that your Higher Power wants only the best for you and all other human beings. You must truly believe that your Higher Power looks at you and thinks, "You rock just because you exist!"

Because of the lasting impact of religious shame, I have found that it is often easier to help an atheist create a concept of a loving Higher Power than it is to help a victim of religious abuse recreate and accomplish the same task. Those old-time religious shame messages have claws that dig deeply into a person's soul and wrap tentacles of self-loathing around a person's heart and mind.

Societal Shame

Societal shame occurs when a group of individuals collectively views others as "less than." This can be done through judgment based on the following:

- Racism
- Sexism
- Homophobia
- Adoration of physical perfectionism

A child who is judged because of his race, gender, sexual orientation, or physical features will start to believe that he was created inferior, bad, or less than. Because a child cannot change how he was created, the child will develop "existence shame" and become toxic to himself. He believes that his very existence is a mistake.

As a result of the child's self-perception that he is defective, the child will feel the need to overcompensate. This is usually done in one of two ways: either the child acts out, thus creating within himself an illusion of power, or the child becomes submissive and attempts to become who he thinks the superior class needs and wants him to be. It is a type of gang mentality. The child or adolescent thinks, *Alone I am nothing. But if I associate with you and your power, I will become something.*

The child throws caution to the wind because the need to belong will override his ability to make decisions that are in his best interest. The defenses against societal judgment cause him to deny the reality of who he is. Self-denial puts the child in a continual state of self-hate and will often create great animosity and aggression toward the self and others.

Personal Relationship/Friendship Shame

As a child begins to socialize, the opinions of peers gain a great deal of importance. Being considered "one of the group" establishes a feeling of internal safety for a child when he is around other children. As social beings, we were created to be in fulfilling relationships. Friendships satisfy our need to belong and add a joyful dimension to life, regardless of age.

If you were ridiculed, teased, or bullied, you were the recipient of personal relationship/friendship shame. This behavior would have been traumatic for you in that your safety (physical and/or emotional) was threatened. Because of the importance of belonging to a peer group and the fear of the offensive behavior escalating, you may have been hesitant to tell a responsible adult about what you were experiencing. As a result, you probably believed that there was no one to rescue you if you needed rescuing. It was scary. In order to compensate for the fear, you may have become shy and antisocial or aggressive toward others. You felt lonely and sad and you just knew that you did not belong.

Chapter Two Exercises:
What You Can Do

- In a notebook or journal, write down ways that as a child you may have experienced any of the types of shame mentioned in this chapter. I want you to start becoming aware of your own childhood experiences. For example:

  a. I felt a lot of pressure from my high school teachers to make straight As every grading period.

  b. My friends used to tease me because I was taller than the other girls.

  c. A neighbor used a slang word when describing my race.

- After each incident, write down how you felt when it happened. For example:

  a. I felt a lot of pressure from my high school teachers to make straight As every grading period. It made me feel angry and overwhelmed.

  b. My friends used to tease me because I was taller than the other girls. It made me feel sad, embarrassed, and scared.

  c. A neighbor used a slang word when describing my race. It made me feel sad, angry, and scared.

- Write a sticky note that says, "I rock because I breathe the air!" Put it in a place where you will see it often. Repeat it to yourself at least twenty times a day.

II

Getting to the Bottom of It:
The Causes and Effects of Shame

Three

"There's a period of life when we swallow a knowledge of ourselves and it becomes either good or sour inside."

—Pearl Bailey—

James had always been his mother's "good boy." As far back as he could remember, James felt obligated to put his mother's wants and needs before his own. Although his basic physical needs were met, James recalled having an overwhelming sense of duty to make his mother happy.

"I mean, I had no choice but to take care of my mother," he explained. "My parents divorced before I was three years old and from that point forward, my father basically disappeared. The worthless son-of-a-bitch made no effort whatsoever to help my poor mom."

"What about you?" I asked James.

"What do you mean, 'What about me?'" James defensively shot back.

I sat in the silence for a moment, letting the intensity in the room subside. "What I mean is: who was there to meet your needs?" I leaned forward and softly responded. "What about that little boy who needed to be nurtured and loved? What was it like for him?"

James looked at the floor, took a deep breath, and sighed. "It just wasn't about me," he said. "There was no one else around to help out my mom. You need to understand. My mom worked long hours and then after work she obviously needed someone to talk to about all of her problems. I was the only one there for her. You know, sometimes there were guys that floated in and out of her life, but they never stayed around for long. No one wanted to take on a kid. Several times a week, I would go with my mom to a bar where she would have a couple of drinks to relax and talk with people, but other than that, I was the one that made her happy. I would give her foot rubs and make dinner for her. My mom was really proud of the way I was always there to take care of her. She used to call me her 'little man.'"

"Are you still your mom's 'little man'?" I asked.

"I guess," answered James. "My wife bitches about it all the time, complaining that whenever my mom calls, I drop everything to take care of her. My wife says that my mom takes precedence over her and my own kids. But you know, that's just the way it has to be. My mom needs me."

James had spent his forty-two years of life taking care of his mother. He had been taught that it was his primary responsibility—his duty—to be his mother's confidant, support system, and source of happiness. James was expected to act beyond his capabilities, which sent him into a perpetual cycle of caretaking his mother. James was unable to be a child because he was too busy being a parent to his mother.

Three

Creating Shame within a Child:

Meet the Parents

Hopefully you now have a working understanding of the meaning of shame, the meaning of self-esteem, and the sources of shame. You may also find yourself buying into the truth of the inherent worth of yourself and others. If you are, then great! If not, hang in there. More will be revealed. At any rate, most people start to ask the question, "How does this distortion of reality take place?" The answer is, "Through ineffective parenting and caregiving."

Ineffective parenting, or the inability of caregivers to root and establish a healthy self-esteem system, leaves a deep wound within a child. Unless the wound is healed, it will remain throughout childhood and continue into adulthood, sustaining the illusion within the individual that he is less valuable than others. This illusion will create a feeling of insecurity and will interfere with his ability to care for self and others.

If your parents had no awareness of their own self-esteem, they simply could not have given you what they were not given when they were children. It is like attempting to pour milk from an empty pitcher. Your parents/caregivers were unable to nurture within you what they did not realize within themselves. Because of that, your needs were never fully met and your self-esteem was never adequately rooted. Thus the woundedness that was formed within your parents was passed down and established within the next generation—you. This generational shame is like a runaway train wreaking internal havoc within family members from generation to generation until someone stops the cycle.

Over time these wounds become larger and result in the creation of a shame core within a child. In other words, a child subconsciously believes to the very core of his being that he is inadequate. This shame core will continue to worsen and will be sustained by the internalization of toxic shame messages. As this happens, the child begins to perceive himself as having very little value. In reality, the child's self-esteem is not lost—it is merely masked.

It is important to remember that one's intrinsic value from birth is absolutely static and permanent. It is the *recognition* of one's value that becomes distorted and lost.

Love does not always equate to effective parenting.

Without a doubt, the great majority of parents, including your parents, do the best job they can possibly do. Their intentions are pure. They believe with all their hearts that they are parenting effectively and with a tremendous amount of love. Unfortunately, love does not always equate to effective parenting. Most people parent as they were parented without realizing that what they are doing is creating emotional wounds deep within the spirit of the child.

As you read about shameful parenting techniques, please focus on yourself as a child as opposed to the ways you may have parented your own children. Remember, the realization of your own woundedness and resulting shame is the beginning of healing. After you connect with yourself as a child, you will then be able to parent your own children differently. If your children are adults, you will be able to make amends to them and help them to break the cycle of generational shame. These deep childhood wounds and the resulting shame core can be formed in the following ways.

Mixed Messages

Mixed messages are created when a parent or caregiver's words and actions are incongruent. This experience is very confusing to a child. Most children do not have the ability or courage to address this incongruence with their caregiver for fear of being considered disrespectful. Many of us grew up being told that it was not OK to question adults. As a result, we learned to dismiss and repress what we were experiencing. We learned to deny our self. Whenever a child's reality is denied, his self-esteem takes a hit. The fallout for the continuation of this sort of experience is an inadequate sense of self-value.

Mixed messages that you may have experienced:
• "You are such a good boy/girl."

If you grew up hearing this statement, you got the message that you had the possibility of being bad. Remember, there is no such thing as a bad child. A more effective statement would be, "You are such a precious child and that can never change." I often hear people refer to a baby that cries as being a bad baby. My body cringes when I hear that statement. It is totally illogical because babies are supposed to cry. It is their only means of communication. Although I realize that the adult does not intend to be offensive, the energy that accompanies the concept of a baby being good or bad depending upon whether the baby sleeps easily or cries is negative. Eliminating the statements that contribute to a negative self-image within a child is an effective way to foster a solid sense of self.

• As a parent is about to discipline the child, he states, "This hurts me more than it does you."

This statement was demeaning to you because it discounted your own pain while it elevated the adult's pain. A more effective statement would be, "I love you very much and I know that you feel sad about being in trouble with me."

Withdrawal of Physical or Emotional Affection

When a parent withdraws physical or emotional affection because of the child's behavior, the child internalizes the message that his unacceptable behavior has reduced his value in the eyes of the parent. Children cannot be responsible for owning their internal value because the total transference from other esteem to self-esteem does not happen until young adulthood. The child must look to the parent or caregiver as his primary source for value validation.

The child believes that if his parents see him as lovable, then he must be lovable. Likewise the child believes that if his parents do not see him as lovable, then he must not be lovable. Withdrawal of affection is read as withdrawal of love. The parent has not separated the child's behavior from his value. This has an extremely damaging effect on the child's solidification and realization of self-esteem.

Examples of physical or emotional withdrawal that you may have experienced:

- Your parent said, "You are very bad for hitting your sister."

  In this situation, your parent was withdrawing emotional nurturing by telling you that you were bad. A nurturing response would be, "Your behavior is not OK and you must stop. You are valuable and precious even though you have misbehaved. Your value can never change."

- Your parent was unwilling to hug you after reprimanding you for unacceptable behavior.

  This sent you a disapproving message of your essence, which you internalized as being less valuable. Although a hug should not be forced upon a child, it is important for a parent to be willing to hug the child even when the parent is unhappy with the child's behavior. A parent can ask the child if he wants a hug or say to the child, "Even though I am angry and I do not like what you have done, I would love to hug you and remind you of your preciousness."

Physical Neglect

Physical neglect can take several forms. Most commonly, it is not meeting the child's need for physical attention or affection. Meeting the child's physical needs determines how the child's body develops and thrives.

Children are incapable of caring for themselves physically so it is vitally important that parents model healthy physical self-care. Habits that are established throughout childhood will be carried into adulthood and will greatly affect a person's physical health throughout his lifetime.

Lovability equates to value.

Equally as important as physical attention is physical affection. If you did not receive a lot of physical affection, you learned to doubt your lovability. Lovability equates to value.

People will say that they know their parents loved them even though they were rarely hugged as children. I always ask them how they knew that they were lovable if their parents did not show them. Remember, children need words and behaviors to be congruent. Even though some adolescents do not like to be hugged, they like for their parents to want to hug them. It is never appropriate, however, to force a child to hug or to be hugged by anyone. Physical neglect also includes not setting appropriate limits for the child. Because children do not naturally set appropriate limits for themselves, a major part of functional parenting is saying no to children when they want to do things that are not in their best interest. A parent's difficulty in setting limits with a child is usually the result of a parent wanting to avoid conflict. A parent can have trouble dealing with their own feelings appropriately and does not want to risk disapproval from the child or adolescent.

To be effective in setting limits, a parent must be able to handle the child's feelings of anger or sadness in having to deal with boundaries. The parent should always operate in the child's best interest, even when the child is resistant. Chances are the child is not going to say, "Gee, Dad. Thanks for persisting in asking me to go to bed." While resistance from children and adolescents is normal and may not be particularly fun, the parent must learn to persevere with setting limits. Children feel valued when they have limits.

Examples of physical neglect that you may have experienced:

- Your parents did not teach you about personal grooming.

    Personal grooming helps a child learn to honor his body by keeping it clean and healthy. As you entered into adolescence, you began to look to your peers rather than your parents for self-validation. Desiring to "fit in" is normal for an adolescent and eliminating body odor, grungy teeth, dirty fingernails, and facial hair (for boys) helps to remove reasons for ridicule and exclusion from peers. Personal grooming is a life skill that the child will take into adulthood, and it will affect his ability to thrive both socially and professionally.

• Your parents did not feed you healthy food and/ or allowed you to overindulge in foods high in fat and sugar.

If left to your own childhood desires, you probably would have lived on greasy french fries and other high-fat foods. Most children will choose pizza over broccoli and ice cream over a glass of milk. Grease and sugar taste good. Teaching a child moderation in regard to eating high-fat and sugary foods will allow the child to enjoy occasional indulgences without becoming controlled by extreme eating behaviors and the potential health issues that may occur as a result. I believe that one of the most covertly abusive behaviors in our culture is a parent allowing a child to eat himself into obesity.

• Your parents did not ensure that you had enough physical activity.

I am not one of those people who believes that television and video games are intrinsically bad. It is important, however, that a child engages in daily moderate physical activity in order to facilitate energy and a sense of well-being.

- Your parents did not set limits on the amount of your physical activities or they pushed you too hard in physical activities.

  There is a trend in our culture of involving children in too many extracurricular sporting activities at the expense of any downtime. Along with activities, it is good for children to learn to relax and do nothing.

- Your parents did not take you to the dentist or doctor.

- Your parents allowed you to stay up as late as you wanted.

  Sleep is essential for growing bodies—and positive attitudes.

Abandonment (Physical and Emotional)

Abandonment is when a parent or caregiver leaves a child physically or is emotionally unavailable.

Physical Abandonment

Children are egocentric in nature and often believe that they are the cause of situations that happen to their parents. For example, if your parents got divorced or separated, you may have assumed that in some way you caused the rift. It is essential that children be told that a parent is not leaving because of the children or the children's behavior.

In the case of a parent's death, the same message applies. This message should be repeated many times. With divorce or separation, it is also extremely important that the parent who is not living with the children take every opportunity to spend time with them. Children need to know that they are loved very much by both parents, that their needs will be met, and that they are safe.

Children may also feel abandoned if one or both parents work away from the home or travel frequently. If this is the case, it is crucial that the children receive nurturing care from whoever takes over for the parents during these times. It is also important for parents to be attentive to the children when the parents are at home, reassuring the children that they are loved very much.

Emotional Abandonment

Emotional abandonment is the unwillingness or inability of a parent to address his own feelings or the feelings of his child. It could be that a parent is denying his own feelings or is so wrapped up in his own emotions that he fails to notice or be sensitive to what is going on with the child.

Examples of emotional abandonment that you may have experienced:

- You saw that your parent was crying, you asked what was wrong, and your parent said, "Nothing is wrong."

    When a parent does not acknowledge the reality of what he is feeling, the child learns to doubt his own reality. The child sees and interprets the obvious and yet his parent denies the obvious. Who is the child to believe, himself or his parent? Parents, in the mind of a child, represent truth and authority. Therefore, the child determines that his truth must be incorrect. This sets up the child for a pattern of self-doubt and negates his ability to trust his gut or birth-created intuition.

An effective response would be, "I am feeling sad. This is my sadness and I will take care of it. It is OK for people to feel sad."

- Your parent noticed that you were feeling sad, fearful, happy, etc., and they did not comment on or talk about your emotions.

  When parents do not notice the feelings of a child, the child feels unloved and will therefore conclude that he must be unlovable. Remember that in order for a child to root healthy self-esteem, he must understand, by seeing and hearing, that his parents regard him as being extremely valuable and lovable. Noticing and verbally acknowledging a child's feelings are effective ways to nurture and root a child's value to the child.

  An effective comment would be, "It looks to me like you are feeling afraid. Can I give you a hug and would you like to talk about it?"

- Your parents did not tell you that they loved you.

  It is *extremely* important that both parents tell children that they love them. Often people will say, "My child knows that I love him even if I don't say it" or "I know that my father or mother loved me although I never heard them say it." Loving actions are absolutely not enough. When parents do not tell their child that they love him, the child will harbor a deep-rooted doubt that he is lovable. A child will hear the words "I love you" spoken between other people and he will subconsciously or consciously question why his parents do not say that to him. The child will easily conclude that there must be something wrong with him to cause his parent not to speak the words, "I love you." Children need to hear the words "I love you" from their parents/ primary caregivers, and they need to hear it often and whole-heartedly!

• Your parent was walled off from his or her own emotions and did not feel, demonstrate, or talk about his emotions.

Emotions are "energy in motion." When a parent does not appropriately acknowledge and feel his emotions, the unacknowledged emotional energy will ooze into the environment rather than disappearing. Because a child is an emotional sponge, he will absorb the emotional energy of the parent, store it internally, claim the emotion as his own, and then feel the emotions of the parent and for the parent. The child may feel these emotions during childhood or later in life, but trust me: they *will* be felt at some time during the child's life.

This often occurs when a parent suffers from depression. Depression is deep sadness, fear, or anger, and even though these feelings have been stuffed and not acknowledged, they are omnipresent in the home environment. The child absorbs the unfelt feelings, internalizes the depressive energy, and develops his own case of depression or anxiety. It is the perfect storm that is recreated within the child. When a client comes into my office and presents with depression or anxiety, I ask which parent or grandparent had depression or anxiety when the client was growing up. We can always trace it back to someone in the family.

The same scenario is true when parents spew their feelings inappropriately into the environment. A child will absorb the spewed feelings, internalize them as his own, and then act them out at some point. Rage is a good example of this. Rage is the behavioral result of accumulated anger that has not been appropriately acknowledged and felt. The anger seethes internally and simply reaches a boiling point. The pressure cooker explodes. As a result, a child will absorb the toxic anger energy and then act it out. People will frequently credit their rage issues to having a "bad temper." It is as if they inherited the temper genetically like the color of their eyes. People are not born with flaring tempers. They absorb flaring toxic energy and then claim it as their own.

On the other hand, a parent who is connected with his own emotional reality and allows himself to experience his emotions without shame will be able to feel his feelings appropriately. This will prevent a child from absorbing the parent's feelings and will also provide a model for appropriate "feeling behavior." For example, a parent who is feeling anger should say to a child, "I am feeling angry. This is my anger, not yours, and I will handle it. It does not mean that I do not love you. I am simply angry."

- Your parents told you that your feelings were wrong and should not be felt, perhaps telling you that you should not cry, feel angry, or feel afraid.

Feelings, or emotions, are a very important part of one's identity, and it is essential that children be allowed to identify and feel their feelings. Feelings that are ignored, shamed, or resisted do not disappear; they actually remain inside one's being and will build upon themselves. As the feelings build, they are then often expressed inappropriately.

When feelings are shamed, a child is shamed. As a defense against the shame, a child will learn to disconnect from his feelings, thus disconnecting from himself. Typically boys are shamed for feeling fear and sadness, while girls are shamed for feeling angry. When feelings are appropriately acknowledged and expressed, however, they will lose power and will not adversely affect a person mentally or physically. Because a child will instinctively express what he is feeling, it is imperative that parents/caregivers teach ways to appropriately express feelings.

An effective parenting statement would be, "It looks like you are feeling sad and that is absolutely all right. Would you like to talk about it?"

Emotional Incest

Emotional incest is using a child to take care of a parent's emotional needs. The child is given the message that their job is to make a parent feel proud, happy, safe, etc. Your parent's job was to take care of your emotional needs by nurturing you with love, validation, and support so that you could focus on age-appropriate activities and relationships.

Emotional incest causes a child to be enmeshed with his parent. This means that there is no separateness. The parent believes that he is a reflection of the child's feelings and behaviors and the child is a reflection of the parent's feelings and behaviors. It is not uncommon for an adult to assume that if his parent committed a crime or committed suicide that he is doomed to a similar behavior. Emotional incest is very detrimental to a child because if a child is parenting his parent, then he is being robbed of his emotional childhood. Not only is the child prevented from being a child emotionally, the parent is not available to focus on parenting the child.

Examples of emotional incest that you may have experienced:

- You misbehaved and your parent made a statement such as, "I feel so disappointed in you. I cannot believe that you would do this to me."

  An appropriate parenting statement would be, "It is not OK to hit your sister and I feel angry. It is my anger and I will deal with it. I do want that behavior to stop."

- Your father said to you, "I am going out of town and you need to take care of your mother and keep her happy."

  An appropriate parenting statement would be, "I am going out of town. Your mom will be here to take care of you. I hope you have a good couple of days."

- Your parents got their feelings hurt because you wanted to spend time with your friends rather than with your parents.

  In this case, you were expected to keep your parents from feeling sad or lonely.

- Your parents expected you to behave in a way that was beyond your capability because of age or cognitive development.

  Your parents needed you to behave in a certain way so that they could feel happy rather than angry or embarrassed. Examples of this are: taking you, as a three-year-old, out to a prolonged dinner and expecting you to sit still and be quiet; expecting you at two years old not to touch items on a coffee table; expecting you and your siblings not to have disagreements; expecting you to be responsible for your siblings.

- Your parents said, "I am so disappointed in you."

  This is an extremely shaming message; it rips the child to the core of his essence. It tells the child that he has failed to fulfill his duty to make his parent feel happy or proud. It is not the child's job to make his parent feel *anything*.

Emotional incest is particularly shame producing because the task set before the child is impossible. Adults are responsible for their own emotional reality. When a child is unable to satisfy a parent's emotional needs, he will feel extremely sad or guilty because he has failed at creating happiness, pride, or love in his parents, the people that he loves the most. That is a monumental job and can produce a lot of fear within the child because he is emotionally and physically dependent on his parents for survival. It is like water-skiing behind a boat that no one is driving! If he cannot please his parents, the child fears possible withdrawal of the attention and love he so desperately needs, thus creating a fear of abandonment that will be carried into adulthood.

Emotional incest also causes a child to feel inadequate and like a failure. It creates the need to be an emotional caretaker, a people pleaser, and a dutiful son/daughter. The child will believe that it is his job to "fix" anyone who is feeling sadness, fear, anger, guilt, or shame. He will absorb the uncomfortable feelings of family and friends, perceive these feelings as being his own, and then make behavioral choices based on the absorbed feelings.

It is never, ever a child's job to take care of a parent emotionally!

The child learns to live life from a place of duty as opposed to living life from a place of choice. These dutiful roles will continue into adulthood and will sabotage the ability to create healthy relationships. People who are overly dutiful will also be unable to feel a general sense of happiness independent from the well-being of others. Their ability to live a satisfying life will be impeded. It is never, *ever* a child's job to take care of a parent emotionally!

Physical Caretaking of a Parent, Grandparent, or Other Adult

Sometimes a child may be used to physically nurture or physically take care of a parent, grandparent, or other adult. This most frequently occurs when the adult suffers from debilitating depression, physical impairment, or chronic mental or physical disease.

Examples of physical caretaking that you may have experienced:

- Your parent or other adult expected you to make him physically comfortable.
- You spent time grooming your parent or other adult by brushing their hair, changing their clothing, bathing them, or changing their adult diaper.
- You spent time sustaining a parent or other adult's health by dispensing their medication or vitamins, exercising them, or taking them to the restroom.
- You gave your parents or other adults foot rubs.
- You fed your parent or other adult.

Like emotional incest, physical caretaking of an adult sets up the child for failure as the task is beyond the child's capability. This does not include a child helping within the family unit or having assigned chores. Chores are more about participating within a system as opposed to feeling responsible for an adult's physical well-being.

An adult may find it necessary to take care of an aging parent or another adult physically. Note that this is different from a child taking care of a parent.

Perfectionism

Perfectionism is a parent's desire for a child to look perfect, act perfectly, and perform perfectly. Even though the parents do not acknowledge their own imperfections or inappropriate behaviors, they expect perfection from a child.

Examples of perfectionism that you may have experienced:

- You brought home a report card with a B+ and your parents complained that you did not make an A.
- You were not allowed to leave the house without your room being perfectly picked up and your bed perfectly made.
- Your parents often fought and yelled at each other, while expecting you and your siblings to always get along and not fight with each other.
- Your parents constantly criticized your physical appearance or insisted that you always look a particular way.

Expecting a child/emerging adult to be perfect impedes him from accepting himself as being real or human. As a result, the child is in a continual state of feeling less than. He becomes like a gerbil in a wheel, always in motion while attempting to do everything better. Because perfection cannot be obtained and sustained, he will learn to do what he perceives he should be doing rather than what he wants to be doing. He becomes frustrated and feels grossly inadequate. He will be hesitant to attempt new endeavors because if he cannot do something perfectly, then he must be a failure. He may also develop a tendency to procrastinate. In order to cope with the shame that results from the inability to achieve perfection, the child learns to focus on and criticize the imperfections of self and others. This character trait will remain throughout adulthood and will sabotage relationships.

Part of being human is doing things imperfectly and learning to do things differently the next time. If a child is taught to exchange the word "mistake" for the words "learning experience," a shameful or negative connotation can be replaced with something positive and esteeming. Pia Mellody calls the concept of embracing our flawed humanity as being created "perfectly imperfect." This is an important part of self-esteem. Children will develop an attitude of self-acceptance by seeing and hearing a parent's self-acknowledgment of his own imperfections as well as the parent giving the child permission to be perfectly imperfect.

Chapter Three Exercises:
What You Can Do

- Whenever you "make a mistake," say to yourself, "I am having a learning experience. I am indeed perfectly imperfect."
- As you continue to learn from your experiences, keep a journal of life lessons that you could not have learned if you had done a task perfectly.
- Keep a log of ways that you expect yourself to be perfect in appearance, work, relationships, and self-care.
- Make a sticky note that says, "I was created perfectly imperfect by divine design." Place it where you will see it often. As you can see, I *love* sticky notes!

Four

"If we were to take a three-year-old child and put her in the middle of the room, and you and I were to start yelling at the child, telling her how stupid she was, how she could never do anything right, how she should do this and shouldn't do that, and look at the mess she made and maybe hit her a few times, we would end up with a frightened little child who sits docilely in the corner or who tears up the place. The child will go one of these two ways, but we will never know the potential of that child."

—Louise Hay—

I do a pretty good job of maintaining a sense of emotional separateness from my clients. Typically I am able to listen to a client's childhood stories without feeling overwhelmed with sadness as I picture him or her as a helpless child. On this particular day, however, it was different.

"It was really terrible watching my parents fight," recalled Monica. "It seems like they fought all of the time."

"What did your parents fight about?" I inquired.

"Everything," responded Monica. "My father would come home after having a few drinks with his buddies, and we *all knew that he would probably explode. One day my mom found a magazine underneath their bed and she was really mad. You know, it was a magazine with nude pictures of women. When she asked my father about it, he went ballistic, calling her all sorts of obscene names. He threw a bunch of stuff in the kitchen and told her that he was going to leave her. If my younger brother or I ever tried to tell him to stop yelling, my father would jerk off his belt and give us a whack or two. He would tell us to mind our own business and call us idiots, telling us we were stupid to think that we had any right to disagree with him about anything."*

"You were probably trying to protect your mom," I said.

"I guess," said Monica. "She seemed so helpless. My father was usually harder on me since I was the oldest. One night, he locked me in a closet and told me that I had to spend the night in there because I asked him to stop calling my brother a crybaby. He kept telling my little brother that he was going to give him something to cry about."

"How old were you?" I asked.

"I was nine," answered Monica. "I was so scared. I was afraid that he might actually kill my mom or little brother. When my mom let me out of the closet the next morning, my father had ripped the heads off all my dolls and had taken my kitten, Fluffy, somewhere away from the house." Monica's voice started to quiver. "At that time, I had no idea what he did with her. A few months later when my father was in another fit of rage, he told me that he drowned Fluffy that night. I couldn't believe that he would do that to me. I had only had her for a few weeks. He knew that little kitten was my very best friend. You know, in an odd way, she made me feel safe. I loved her so much."

My heart was aching for Monica. I tried to pull myself together as my eyes filled with tears. "Did your father ever say 'I'm sorry' after one of those terrible nights?" I asked.

"Not really," replied Monica. "But when I turned about thirteen, he would get in bed with me after one of their fights and try to snuggle with me."

My stomach knotted as I began to imagine what happened to Monica in that bed. "Monica, did your father touch your body anywhere that felt uncomfortable?" I questioned.

Monica looked at me with tears streaming down her cheeks. "Yes," she sobbed. "I would lie there frozen and pretend to be asleep so that he would not get angry. It was so horrible and I felt so dirty. I have never told anyone about this because I was so embarrassed. I always felt like it was something I had done wrong, like I had caused it. It just makes me sick."

I sat in silence for several minutes, allowing Monica to release the incredible amount of pent-up sadness that she had kept inside for twenty years.

"I am so sorry that you experienced that as a young girl, Monica. All of those things that your father did were wrong. It was wrong for him to yell and throw things. It was wrong for him to hit you and your brother with a belt. It was wrong for him to call you names and take your kitten. And it was especially wrong for your father to touch you like that," I explained. "Monica, it was not your fault. Your father was a very sick man. I am really glad that you were able to finally let go of that terrible secret. We will work through this together so that you can live your life free from the bondage of the abuse. Thank you for feeling safe enough with me to talk about it."

Four

The Impact of Abuse:

Through the Eyes of a Child

Child abuse is the mistreatment of a child—physically, emotionally, or intellectually. Of course there are varying degrees of abuse, some more extreme than others, but regardless of the circumstances, it is important to remember that child abuse is always damaging to a child. An adult abusing a child is absolutely never OK. It does not matter whether the adult experienced abuse as a child himself or considers the abusing behavior normal or acceptable.

Abuse is abuse and it is always unacceptable.

It is a parent's job to nurture a child and make him feel loved and safe. This simply cannot happen in the presence of abuse. When a child does not feel safe, either physically, emotionally, or intellectually, the child will develop defense mechanisms in order to equip himself with the capacity to tolerate his stress and anxiety. Sigmund Freud and other theorists have identified a number of defense mechanisms such as denial, repression minimization, justification rationalism, and fantasy, just to name a few. All of the defense mechanisms that are employed by a child will be taken into adulthood and will impede the adult in his ability to live from a place of emotional maturity. Take fantasy, for example. If an adult looks at life through the lenses of fantasy, he will have great difficulty seeing situations as they really are. When the facts of a situation do not match reality, he will change the facts of a situation to match his fantasy rather than changing his fantasy to match reality. He cannot live in truth and will make decisions based on his fantasy.

If one parent is the primary abuser and the other parent sits silently by watching the abuse, the silent parent is in collusion with the overt abuser. He is a covert abuser and is actually participating in the abuse. It is always a parent's job to intervene on behalf of the child *whenever* abuse (and shame) is apparent.

As you read about the types of behaviors that constitute abuse, think about what you experienced as a child. *Try to keep yourself from minimizing your own experience by comparing it to what could have happened or what you know happened to others.*

In addition, you as a child did not have the capacity to fully differentiate your own experiences from the experiences of others. A child witnessing the abuse of another child or adult is also abused.

The following definitions of abuse are from Pia Mellody's workshops at The Meadows in Wickenburg, Arizona.

Verbal Abuse

Verbal abuse includes:

- Name-calling—Some forms of verbal abuse are more overtly abusive than others. It is easy for most people to see that calling a child an idiot is abusive, but you may not realize that being called stupid, worthless, a sissy, a crybaby, or a brat is abusive as well. Name-calling is not OK. Parents should never call a child a derogatory name, and they should intervene if they ever witness such an action. Parents should also insist that siblings not call each other names.

- Yelling and screaming—If anyone yelled or screamed at you (or anyone else in front of you), it was abusive. It does not matter if it was your parent, another family member, teacher, or another individual. Yelling and screaming should not be allowed in any home, under any circumstance. We tend to teach children that they should tolerate yelling from adults out of respect for the adults. I think this is absolutely ludicrous. If we teach our children to tolerate verbal abuse, they will develop a tolerance muscle for abuse. They will be much more likely to tolerate abuse from a future partner or be abusive themselves. Children desperately need to learn that they should have a zero tolerance muscle for being the recipient of abuse as well as the perpetrator of abuse.

- Not responding to or ignoring a child—Ignoring or not speaking to a child out of frustration, hurt, or as a form of punishment may not appear to be abusive, but it is considered to be covert verbal abuse and is extremely damaging to a child. It is a form of emotional abandonment. Being ignored by your parent was confusing to you and it made you feel unsafe.

  If a parent is feeling really angry and is afraid that they will yell at a child, they should say something like, "I am feeling really angry right now so I am going to be quiet for a few minutes so that I can breathe through this anger. I will talk with you about this in a few minutes. These are my feelings, and it is my job to deal with them."

  Your parents may have also withdrawn into a silent pout when they felt hurt about something you did or said. I have heard many parents say, "How could my child do this to me?" When a parent feels hurt by the child, the parent has personalized the child's behavior and is acting like a child himself. Children do not do things to parents; they simply do things.

- Sarcasm and teasing that is intended to mock or ridicule—"Sarcasm" comes from the Greek word "*sarcazo*," which means "to tear the flesh." Like other forms of verbal abuse, sarcasm can be either overt or covert. Overt sarcasm would include a cutting remark or spiteful innuendo, while a scornful sneer would be considered covert sarcasm. You may be saying to yourself, "My parents were just teasing when they used sarcasm," but it was virtually impossible for you to differentiate a harmless tease from a putdown.

My father was raised on a ranch in Texas and was one of seven children—six boys and one girl. He was the only one of the children who attended college as an adult and continued to live away from his place of birth.

When I was a little girl, my family would visit my father's family five or six times a year. I loved visiting my grandmother and playing with my cousins (there were nineteen of us), but I absolutely hated the times when all my uncles were around. They would tease me mercilessly, which more often than not resulted in me feeling terribly embarrassed and bursting into tears. My reaction to their teasing only spurred them on as they called me "crybaby" and told me I was too "thin skinned."

I remember one incident in particular when my sister chased me with a firecracker. I was probably five years old and I was terrified. I started crying and screaming, and my uncles thought my response was hilarious. As I listened to them mock my crying and call me a crybaby, I desperately looked around for my father to rescue me. My father simply stood in the circle with his brothers and chuckled. Although I now understand that their intentions were not to shame me, the impact of their behavior was profoundly shaming. As I am writing this story, my stomach tightens and I feel angry and sad that no one intervened on behalf of that precious little girl.

Most uses of sarcasm and teasing feel like a putdown and are hurtful to an adult, let alone to a child. Sarcasm and excessive teasing undermine a child's concept of their value and should be avoided when speaking to a child or another adult.

- A child witnessing the verbal abuse of another child or adult.

Physical Abuse
Physical abuse includes:
- Spanking with an object
- Face slapping
- Shaking
- Hair pulling
- Tickling into hysteria
- Pinching
- Allowing a child to witness or hear the physical abuse of another child or adult

---

Our prisons are full of people who were spanked and disciplined using various forms of physical punishment. It simply does not work.

Although your parents may have believed that spanking you was the only way to get you to stop a particular behavior, history has shown that it does not work. Our prisons are full of people who were spanked and disciplined using various forms of physical punishment. It simply does not work. We rightly tell children at a very early age that it is not OK to hit other people and yet we hit our children with an air of self-justification. Do you see how incongruent this is? How can it possibly be OK for a parent or anyone else to hit a child?

Most parents who use forms of physical punishment do so from a place of intense anger. The parents transfer their own anger or rage onto the body of their child. The child then internalizes the rage and will act out toward himself or others. If a child can be so "bad" as to cause his parents this amount of angst, he will question how he can possibly have any internal value. Spanking is often the easiest way to discipline and has been called the "lazy man's tool for parenting." I strongly advise my clients *not* to spank their children.

Sexual Abuse

Sexual abuse includes:

- Intercourse (including anal sex)
- Oral sex
- Masturbation
- Sexual touching (fondling)
- Sexual kissing
- Sexual hugging
- Voyeurism
- Exhibitionism
- Verbal sexual trauma (telling sexual jokes in front of the child)

- Failure to have sexual boundaries in front of the child (including a child hearing sexual activity)
- The child witnessing sexual abuse to another child or adult

Being sexually abused as a child is a deeply shameful experience. Because children are egocentric in nature, they believe that they must somehow be partially responsible for the abuse. Often the abuser is a family member. Out of loyalty to the family member and because of the deep level of shame that resulted from the sexually abusive experience, the child typically keeps the experience to himself. Since sexual abuse can take many forms, victims of abuse often minimize or repress the experience in an effort to cope. The internal shame, which is tremendous, festers deep within the soul of the child, eroding any sense of self-value.

All forms of sexual abuse are damaging and will have a lasting impact. When a child develops into adulthood, these experiences will often negatively affect their ability to embrace their own healthy sexuality. It can also hinder their ability to have healthy intimate sexual relationships. The effects of sexual abuse may result in promiscuity, deviant sexual behavior, or a complete lack of sexual interest.

Intellectual Abuse
Intellectual abuse includes:
- Attacking the child's thinking process
- Overcontrolling the expression of a child's thoughts
- Failing to teach logical thinking and problem solving

Many parents tell their children that they should not think a particular way. What a child thinks, at any age, about a particular subject comprises a large portion of the child's sense of self. If you were shamed for your thought process or not encouraged to think and problem solve for yourself, you internalized the shame and applied it to all parts of yourself. It is simply impossible for a child to value himself if his primary caregivers do not value his ability to think. There will be times, of course, when a parent disagrees with a child. It is not abusive for a parent to state that he disagrees with what a child is thinking or to express hope that a child takes on a similar belief about an issue. This can and should be done without demeaning a child and his beliefs.

Examples:

- You said to your parent, "Billy pushed me down and said I was ugly. I told Billy he was mean." In response, your parent said, "You shouldn't think like that or say those things to people." Your parent was trying to control what you were thinking. An appropriate response from your parent would have been," Let's talk about why you think that about Billy. It looks to me like you are really angry about how Billy treated you."

- As an adolescent, you stated that you think teenagers should not have a curfew. Your parent reacted by telling you that you were crazy and stupid for thinking that way. An effective parenting response would have been, "I understand why you think teenagers are old enough to not have a curfew. I probably thought the same thing at your age. Although I understand your thinking, I do not agree with it and because I am your parent, I am going to require you to be in at a particular time."

Spiritual/Religious Abuse

Spiritual abuse includes:

- Religious addiction of the parent or primary caregiver
- Trauma at the hands of a religious caregiver
- A parent acting like he or she is a god or goddess of the family

Your religious system may have delivered traumatizing messages that taught you that you were born intrinsically bad. You may have been told that as an individual you had to earn your way into the graces of God by believing in one particular truth. If this was your experience, it may be enormously difficult to undo the damage that was created when you were taught that at birth you fell short of the mark.

My own childhood experience may be of some value in explaining what it was like to be raised with religious abuse. I spent the first ten years of my life in a small West Texas town. My father owned the newspaper and my mother was a stay-at-home mom.

We attended a fundamentalist, evangelical church that was the center of activity for our family. We attended church every time the doors were open. On Sunday morning, we went to Sunday school for an hour followed by worship service for another hour. On Sunday afternoon from 5:00 p.m. until 6:00 p.m., I participated in choir practice. After choir practice, I went to training union, which was like a Bible study, for an hour and then we went to an evening worship service that would last from an hour to an hour and a half. On Wednesday nights, we attended another hour-long worship service. If the church was having a weeklong revival, we would attend a service every night of the week. In the summer, I attended Vacation Bible School every day for two weeks. As you can see, a lot of time was spent in our church.

During church services, my family sat in the second or third row directly in front of the preacher. I vividly remember the preacher pounding the podium with his fist and yelling about how all humans were born with a terrible "sin nature." The preacher yelled about people being evil and how the devil could mess with a person's mind, tempting a person to sin. If a person sinned (and of course sin was inevitable because of our "sin nature"), then God was sad and disappointed. I remember hearing that our sin separated us from God.

In a loud, booming voice, the preacher would rail about how each of us would "burn in hell for eternity" if we did not become "saved." At the end of the service, the preacher invited those who wanted to be saved to come to the front of the church, confess their sins, and agree to a particular set of beliefs. Anyone, absolutely anyone, who did not believe in what the preacher was saying, was doomed to spend eternity with the devil in a fiery hell. I spent hours sitting in that pew between my parents feeling very frightened of God's wrath and like I was a terrible person. I thought that God was a tyrant and that He was just waiting for me and other people to mess up.

Needless to say, I tried to do exactly what the preacher told us to do. I memorized Bible verses, competed for any award that was available through the church, and even told a friend of mine whose family did not attend church that her whole family was in trouble with God. I certainly did not want to burn in hell when I died, and I was terribly worried about others and what they believed. At age eight, I walked down the aisle at the end of a church service, crying my eyes out, and told that preacher that I believed everything he said. Church was a *very* scary place with *very* scary messages.

As opposed to believing that my preciousness and value were created at birth, I believed that I was born with little or no value. I believed that I was expected to "do it right" so that I could gain favor in the eyes of my Creator. The world is a very scary place if a child thinks that believing the right thing or doing the right thing will determine his place for eternity.

A child should be taught to embrace his imperfection as a part of the divinely designed human experience.

Rather than hating his imperfection and striving to attain favor, a child should be taught to embrace his imperfection as a part of the divinely designed human experience. Sin, or being created imperfect, does not separate us *from* our Creator; rather it drives us *to* our Creator, to a universal love.

In my opinion, spiritual/religious abuse is the most difficult to repair because it is rooted in the very soul of one's being. Its tentacles reach into all facets of life, crushing one's spirit and eliminating spontaneity and the possibility of joy. The damaging messages undermine a person's ability to love one's self and therefore one's ability to truly love others. Shame thrives on religious abuse.

Chapter Four Exercises:
What You Can Do

- At the top of an index card write "Physical Abuse." Start to think of ways that you may have been physically abused as a child up to the age of eighteen, either by a parent, another caretaker, a relative, a teacher, sibling, friend, or anyone else. As you think of situations when you were abused, briefly write them on the card. If you are not sure whether or not the person's behavior was abusive, go ahead and put it down. Do not let yourself defend the person by rationalizing, minimizing, or justifying their actions. This is about you and what you experienced.

    a. Repeat the same process on four additional cards headed "Verbal Abuse," "Sexual Abuse," "Intellectual Abuse," and "Spiritual/Religious Abuse." Put these cards in your journal or in this book for future reference.

    b. The intention of this exercise is to begin the process of connecting with yourself as a child.

- When you're out in public, take note if you see an adult abusing a child in any way, imagining how that child might be feeling. Imagine yourself as a child having the same experience.

Five

"I looked in the mirror and knew not who that
person was. All I knew was that the person in the
mirror returned my gaze with loathing."

—Author unknown—

For the past twenty years, Michael had been living
the American dream. He had a thriving business, a
wonderful family, and the adoration of his friends. When
Michael came to see me, however, everything had changed. On
the brink of bankruptcy and divorce, Michael decided that
he needed help.

I knew that Michael was angry when I first saw him
sitting in the lobby of my office. His face was red and his
right heel was tapping rapidly. As I introduced myself and
shook his hand, I noticed that his palm was sweaty. "Wow,"
I thought. "This guy is about to implode."

The moment Michael sat down in my office, he began
talking. "I just don't get it," he said. "My life is spiraling out
of control. It is like a runaway freight train that is headed
toward a mountain that has no tunnel."

"What's going on specifically?" I asked.

"Well, first of all," Michael angrily responded, "my wife
told me three days ago that she wanted me to move out. I

mean, can you believe that? I have literally worked twelve-hour days just to provide her and the kids with everything they could possibly want. And to make matters worse, I am on the verge of freaking bankruptcy."

"Why does your wife want you to leave the house?" I asked.

"Who the hell knows?" Michael answered. "She says that she is tired of my moodiness, my drinking, and my carousing. It's like I tell her, anyone under the stress that I am under would need to release some tension."

"What are you doing that your wife calls carousing?" I questioned.

"You know, just what every other guy that walks the earth does," explained Michael defensively. "Sometimes after a stressful day at work, I might meet some friends or colleagues at a bar for a couple of scotch and waters. I don't do it every night. The problem is my wife doesn't even want me to drink much at home. She says that my 'buzz' isn't good for our relationship because I get so moody with her and the kids. She just doesn't get what it's like to feel so much pressure."

I had a feeling that there was more to the story. "Where do you and your friends go to have a drink?" I asked. "Do you go to gentlemen's clubs?"

"Yeah, but only a couple of times a month," Michael explained. "It's not like there is anything wrong with it. Like I tell my wife, all guys do it. It is just a little harmless fun."

Michael continued, "That's not even the worst of it. Along with all of the grief that my wife is giving me, my business is about to tank. This business has been in our family for two generations. My father would literally roll over in his grave if he knew what was happening. He started grooming me to take it over when I was fourteen. I used to work there in the summer and it was the one thing that made my father proud of me."

"Tell me what it was like working for your father," I said.

"Man, it was great," said Michael. "It was so cool being the boss's son. After work, I got to hang out with my father and his employees, drinking beer and chasing women. My friends thought I was really lucky. I don't know what I will do if I lose this business. Sometimes I think life wouldn't be worth living. It's all I've got. It's who I am."

Everything that had previously defined Michael was vaporizing before his very eyes. His externalized sense of self that had worked so well for him in the past was no longer working. Michael found himself on a downward spiral headed for self-destruction and despair.

Five

The Effects of Shame:

Your Own Personalized Downward Spiral

When a toxic shame core has been created, it is impossible for healthy self-esteem to become rooted. You start to perceive yourself as being inadequate, incomplete, and emotionally unsafe. It is as if a cavernous void exists deep within your soul. In an effort to fill the illusionary hole and feel good about yourself, you begin to seek esteem and security in alternate ways. You create a substitute—or externalized—sense of self for your absent self-esteem.

When this shame core emerges in childhood, the ways in which you learn to externalize your value actually become survival techniques, providing a way for you to suppress the toxic shame. You are able to seemingly fill your esteem tank, creating an illusion of self-value and safety. The illusion will not last, however, and will not provide long-term satisfaction or fulfillment.

An externalized sense of self simply cannot do what you need it to do—give you value. Because it offers relief and is practiced over many years, the externalized sense of self will struggle for self-preservation and will be carried into adulthood. That sense of self will continue to gain importance, momentum, and resistance to change.

You may find yourself in a continuous search for something to make you feel fulfilled or valuable.

If you were raised in a shame-based system, you may find yourself in a continuous search for something to make you feel fulfilled or valuable. You may be looking on the outside for something to make you feel better on the inside. I, too, spent many years pursuing one thing or another, looking for that elusive feeling of self-satisfaction. I was trying to find the one thing that would make me happy and content with me being me. Of course, all I needed to do was realize that "me being me" was enough!

The following are examples of ways you may have learned to externalize your value:

- **Money/possession esteem**—You have value because you have a particular sum of money or own particular items.

- **Professional/work esteem (staying busy, busyness)**—You have value because you have a particular career or participate in particular activities.

- **Relationship esteem**—You have value because you are in a relationship with a particular person. This can be a significant other, a friend, or a parent or child. (In a parent/child relationship, the parent may also gain value because of their child's accomplishments. Using that relationship for self-esteem restricts the parent from setting appropriate limits and consequences for the child.)

- **Looks/vanity esteem/body image**—You have value because of your physical appearance. This can be beauty, youth, or body type.

- **Education esteem**—You have value because you attended a particular educational institution or completed a particular level of education.

- **Religious esteem**—You have value because you ascribe to particular religious beliefs or attend a particular religious institution. Religiosity is very different from spirituality. Spirituality, or the realization of your connection to others and a Higher Power, is the cornerstone of self-esteem. Spirituality is embracing the concept that your value was established at birth and therefore can never be altered in any way. Religiosity, in contrast, is ascribing to a particular institutionalized scheme of beliefs and practices that relate to a Divine Being. Of course it is possible to practice a particular religion and also be spiritual. It is also possible for a person to be religious and have no true sense of spirituality.

- **Performance esteem**—You have value because you perform well at particular tasks or accomplish particular deeds.

- **Power esteem**—You have value because you have power over individuals or because of your reputation or notoriety. Examples of those with power esteem may include politicians, religious figures, corporate leaders, and celebrities.

Interestingly enough, society accepts many of these as suitable replacements for self-esteem and often embraces and encourages them as normal, successful living. When you externalize your value in these forms, however, you are creating a precarious false sense of self-esteem, which can never fully solidify and can quickly disappear. For example, you could lose your job, lose a relationship, or lose your youthful appearance. If you have placed your self-value externally and then lose that entity, you will most likely feel less than, worthless, and terribly inadequate. The loss can be so devastating to your perception of self-esteem that you could become clinically depressed. I see it happen all of the time. The pain that accompanies feeling inadequate can be intense and overwhelming.

It is important to understand that none of these externalized forms of self-esteem are intrinsically bad within themselves. Only when they provide the source of internal value for the individual do they become a threat to the self.

Self-esteem is like a beautifully iced cake. The cake is the essence of the delicacy, while the icing is used to add flavor and aesthetic appeal. Without the cake (true self-esteem), the icing (externalized forms of self-esteem) has no foundation; it cannot stand alone.

You can determine for yourself whether or not you have externalized your sense of self-esteem by asking yourself if you need a particular thing in order to feel value or if you simply want it because the thing or its attainment brings you pleasure. This is a matter of need versus want. Of course, the loss of something material or the loss of a relationship may cause you to feel anger, fear, or pain. That is a natural human response to loss. But if you are overwhelmingly devastated and feel worthless because of the loss, you have probably ascribed your self-esteem to whatever was lost.

Medicating Toxic Shame

Unresolved toxic shame is emotionally painful and will cause a person to develop a shame-based approach to life. Decisions will be made out of shame and sustained joy will be unattainable. As a result, a person may find the need to medicate or numb his pain. Because the numbing process will not last, he may find himself needing more of whatever he has used to medicate his discomfort. *The desire to feel different is insatiable.* A person's relationships, job, education, health, and financial prosperity can be affected. As the numbing process progresses, it often develops into an addiction. An addiction is defined as a psychological and/or physical dependency on a substance or behavior. It includes tolerance and a compulsion to repeat a behavior despite negative consequences.

The following behaviors are potential addictions that you may be experiencing:

- **Alcohol and drug addiction**—Drinking alcohol moderately and using prescription drugs as prescribed are not considered addictions.

- **Food addictions (overeating, anorexia, bulimia)**—Shame feels like a perpetual emptiness and can be confused with hunger. Because the need for food is instinctual and necessary, you can easily use it as a means to medicate or numb your shame.

- **Sex addiction**—Like food, the desire for sex is instinctual. Sexual acts within your value system do not constitute an addiction unless there are negative consequences for yourself or others. Excessive use of pornography is considered a sex addiction. Child pornography and adult sexual acts with a minor are never acceptable.

- **Nicotine dependency**—Nicotine is considered to be an immensely powerful drug with extremely damaging consequences. Although you may think that nicotine calms the anxiety associated with shame, it is actually a stimulant that increases anxiety.

- **Gambling addiction**—The availability of online gambling has brought about a substantial rise in gambling addiction, especially in young adults. If you gamble, watch out for the "high" and the feeling of a need for more.

- **Relationship addiction**—Being in a relationship can be rewarding and satisfying. If you have a chronic need for a relationship as a means of validating your lovability, you may be flirting with a possible relationship addiction.

- **Power addiction (politicians, ministers, celebrities, therapists)**—Power addictions occur when you crave the accolades of others in order to feel acceptable to yourself.

- **Work/activity addiction (busyness)**—Excessive work and activities are ways that you may busy yourself out of your feelings of shame. You may have difficulty being still because when you are still, you feel the restlessness and pain of shame.

- **Spending/possession addiction**—This addiction is particularly susceptible to the insatiability of shame. The relief that you feel through spending and the accumulation of possessions is very short-lived. The more you get, the more you want.

- **Religious addiction**—If you are a religious addict, you will have great difficulty sitting in your humanness because your humanness is bad. You will only feel adequate when you are involved in a religious endeavor or seeking a more mountaintop religious experience.

- **Controlling and caretaking others**—Controlling and caretaking at the expense of yourself is a shame-based way in which you can completely take yourself out of yourself. When focusing on others, it is impossible to focus on what you are feeling or what you may need to change in order to make your life work for you.

Specifically, as you continue to pursue measures beyond yourself to "feel better," the process of self-destruction is only further fed. Chaotic and unbalanced behaviors make it impossible to recognize self-esteem. If you continually experience negative consequences as the result of the unbalanced behaviors, toxic shame only increases.

---

*To put it simply, the love of others is the
extension and overflow of self-love or self-esteem.*

When you live within the confines of a shame core, love and joy are impossible. To put it simply, the love of others is the extension and overflow of self-love or self-esteem, and joy is experienced as you feel love for yourself and others.

Chapter Five Exercises:
What You Can Do

• Make a list of the ways that you have learned to externalize your sense of self. Did you learn money/possession esteem or relationship esteem? Maybe it was looks esteem or education esteem. You may determine that you have developed several different forms of externalized value. That is absolutely normal and OK. This is for your own awareness. If you feel *any* shame at all, throw it away and tell yourself that you are precious. You are in the process of change and change takes courage. You should actually be given a medal of honor!

• Now make a list of any possible addictions that may be impeding your ability to thrive and live from a place of joy. Again, *no shame.* As you continue in the process of healing your shame, you will probably find yourself wanting to let go of behaviors that no longer work. Some will start to fall away; for others, you can seek help in determining an appropriate course of action.

III

Healing the Wounded Child:
It's Time to Baby Yourself

Six

"In the infinity of life, where I am,
all is perfect, whole, and complete.
I am always Divinely protected and guided.
It is safe for me to look within myself.
It is safe for me to look into the past.
It is safe for me to enlarge my viewpoint of life.
I am far more than my personality—
past, present, or future.
I now choose to rise above my personality problems
To recognize the magnificence of my being.
I am totally willing to learn to love myself.
All is well in my world."

—Louise Hay—

*H*eather was born in a small town in Kansas and had *a sister who was three years younger than her. Her father owned the town's radio station and worked long hours, which often included weekends. When Heather's father did not work on Saturday, he played golf at the country club with his friends. Although Heather's father had an outgoing personality and was happy most of the time, he did not talk about feelings or life choices with his daughters. He needed and expected Heather's mother to be happy since he was such a good provider.*

Heather's mother was quite beautiful, very slim, and involved in many civic activities. She looked like the perfect wife and mother. She was always perfectly groomed and well mannered, and expected her two daughters to look and behave perfectly. The family belonged to an evangelical church, which they attended several times a week.

Heather and her sister were typical children, often bickering and disagreeing with one another. Heather was the more rambunctious of the two and would often pick on her younger sister, making her cry. When this occurred, Heather's mother would become extremely upset, yelling at the girls and spanking them with a wooden spoon. If Heather really acted "badly," her mother would call her husband home from work so that he could discipline Heather by spanking her with a belt. The only time Heather experienced her father's rage was when he disciplined her for upsetting her mother.

The children's behavior would overwhelm Heather's mother, sometimes triggering a period of depression during which she would stay in bed and attend to only the essential caregiving of her children. As she retreated into her world of silence, gloom, and seething anger, she resented her husband for not rescuing her from her depression. When Heather's mother could pull herself out of a depressive episode, she would again focus on her daughters looking and acting perfectly and would submerge herself in civic and church activities, once again presenting to the world the perfect family.

As a way to seek her parent's forgiveness and approval for being a bad girl, Heather learned to perform. She became an overachiever and sought perfection in all of her activities. Heather put pressure on herself to make straight As in school and thrived on competition, entering spelling bees, piano *competitions, singing competitions, and contests at church. Heather was often named as the teacher's helper because of her ability to make good grades but was teased by her peers for being the teacher's pet. She was also teased for having crooked teeth and freckles.*

When Heather entered middle school, she got braces and was greatly relieved that her freckles started fading. She then began to seek perfection in her appearance, believing that it was imperative that she dress impeccably and maintain a very low body weight. After having her first boyfriend in eighth grade, it became extremely important that Heather always be in a relationship. It was also essential that she be part of the popular crowd, be elected to student council, and become a cheerleader.

Heather continued to seek perfection throughout high school and graduated first in her class, an accomplishment that made her parents extremely proud.

Throughout her childhood and adolescence, everything appeared to be great for Heather. Inside, however, she experienced great emotional pain. As Heather entered high school, she became obsessed with being skinny, evaluating every calorie that went into her mouth. She often had stomachaches and overwhelming anxiety. In order to relieve her anxiety, she exercised obsessively, worked harder in school, started drinking alcohol, and needed a boyfriend at all times. She was the perfect girlfriend, never asking for anything and tolerating her boyfriend's yelling and infidelity. Heather attended the college of her father's choice, graduated with honors, and married her long-term sweetheart.

Heather and her husband moved to a large city and had four daughters. Her husband became quite successful in commercial real estate and he and Heather involved themselves in civic activities. Like her mother, Heather expected excellent behavior, perfect grooming, and perfect manners from her children. Her husband had extremely high academic expectations of the children and often spanked the girls for misbehaving. Heather attended a fundamentalist church where she was always involved in a Bible study. She restricted her diet to two light meals a day so that she could maintain her low body weight, overexercised, and busied herself with many political and social activities.

As Heather's husband achieved greater financial success, he often entertained clients with elaborate dinners and visits to strip clubs. He frequently stayed out very late drinking with his buddies. If Heather complained, he would yell at her, call her names, and tell her that she was crazy and should be grateful for all that he had provided.

Heather became depressed. Rather than attending to her children's emotional and sometimes physical needs, she obsessed about her husband's activities. She prayed that her husband would stop drinking, as her minister told her that God would not tolerate divorce. She was told that if she prayed hard enough, God would either "get" her husband sober or God would give her the strength to stay in the marriage. Heather developed a variety of physical ailments, and after twelve years of prayer and nineteen years of marriage, she felt hopeless. Heather finally came to the conclusion that the only answer was getting out, and the only way out was suicide.

Fortunately, Heather had some very good friends who recognized that she was in trouble. They took her to dinner and lovingly told her that they were worried about her. They gave her my name and suggested that she contact me as soon as possible. Heather heeded her friends' advice.

Six

Weeding Out the Negative:

Eliminate Shame from the Root

Now that you have gained an understanding of shame and the ways that shame has affected your life, you are ready to begin the process of healing your childhood wounds.

Although you may have previously recognized unhealthy behaviors and wanted to do things differently, you could have found yourself unable to make or sustain the desired changes. You are not weak and you are not inadequate; that is just the essence of the shame game. You make a move to do things differently and you may see progress for a period of time, but the changes do not last. The same or similar issues rear their ugly heads again, only to create more difficulties accompanied by more feelings of guilt and shame. Shame has made its move, and shame always wins this game.

So why can you not achieve your expected and desired level of transformation and improvement?

---

*Lasting change and abundant living simply
cannot coexist in the presence of shame.*

The reason for this is that you have not gotten to the root of your shame. You have been altering circumstances and behaviors on the surface rather than destroying the shame completely. Shame is like a bothersome weed in a garden. If only the top of the weed is removed, the weed will grow back, become larger, and possibly spread. The weed has to be removed from the root in order to be eliminated. Perhaps you have experienced a drug or alcohol addiction. You may no longer drink alcohol, but instead you have developed an addiction to sex, coffee, nicotine, or something else. Perhaps you have been addicted to being in a relationship. The dysfunctional relationship may have ended, but you find yourself addicted to pornography, excessive spending, religion, or obsessive-compulsive behaviors. Without uprooting the shame core, you will be unable to embrace your inherent value. Lasting change and abundant living simply cannot coexist in the presence of shame.

So where is the shame root and what is the most effective way for the woundedness to be healed?

The root of the shame lies in the soul and heart of that precious and incredibly powerful wounded child (you). As the child experienced shame from his caregivers, developed a shame core, and then created or internalized behaviors to deal with the shame, the resulting woundedness set up residence within the child. This shame-core woundedness and resulting behaviors have been rooting and growing since their creation. As a result, you become reactive to life events and develop certain life attitudes that become second nature. For example, you may say, "I have a really bad temper. I just can't help it." You justify this rage as if it were somehow in your genetic makeup. Rage, however, is a learned behavior that protects you from feeling uncomfortable feelings such as fear, sadness, anger, guilt, or shame. It is not simply in your DNA. You *learned* to rage from a rage-full, shame-based parent or other caregiver. Your shame-filled parent either raged with overt anger or seethed with covert anger from his own woundedness. Your parent then modeled this behavior that you, as a shame-filled child, readily accepted. You had no capacity to filter and then discard those childhood experiences that were nonfunctional. To you, these experiences were normal—it's all you knew. As a result, you internalized the messages and then reacted to life from the same point of reference as your parent or caregiver. This is largely why children who are physically, verbally, or sexually abused tend to grow up and become abusers or pick abusive partners.

Because the shame root lies within a wounded child, it is necessary to uproot the shame by reparenting the child. Reparenting the wounded child with compassion is the essence and sole purpose of the healing process. When you, as an adult, reparent the wounded child that lives deep within your being, you will recognize your birth-created value and begin to live life free from shame. As emotional maturity develops within your adult self, you will shift from a child-like emotional state to a healthy adult emotional state. You will allow yourself to be imperfect, practice self-care, and live moderately. You will allow yourself to feel feelings and leave abusive relationships. You will begin to experience abundance because you now believe that you deserve abundance. You are basically giving yourself what you were not given from your primary caregivers: nurturing love.

Chapter Six Exercises:
What You Can Do

- Set a timer for five minutes. Sit in a quiet room, close your eyes, and see if you can pull up a mental picture of yourself as a child somewhere between the ages of three and ten. What are you wearing? What color is your hair? How is your hair styled? What are you doing? Do you like that child or do you feel contempt for that child? Continue to think about that child until the timer buzzes.

- When you get into your car, pretend that the child you pictured in the above exercise is riding in the car with you. Make sure you see that child safely buckled in a seat belt or in a car seat. Talk to that child in a loving way, telling him that you are glad to have him with you. Tell him that you have missed him and that you will never leave him. Take note of the feelings that arise for you during this exercise.

Seven

"I look in the mirror through the eyes
of the child that was me."

—Judy Collins—

"How are you doing?" I asked Stephen. "Were you able to connect with that precious little boy that you showed me in your childhood pictures?"

"At first when I started talking to myself in the pictures, I felt like a total dork," answered Stephen. "I was really glad that no one could hear me. This is a pretty cheesy process, you know."

"Yes, I know," I said. "I actually felt rather silly myself when I first started trying to connect with my little girl pictures. Trust me; it gets easier all the time. Now I love looking at myself as a child and telling her how precious she is."

"I did get better at it as the week moved along," stated Stephen. "I didn't have any trouble loving myself as a four-year-old. He looked really cute and he looked like he needed me. But there was one of the pictures that I just could not stand to look at."

"Which one was that?" I asked.

"It was the picture of me in a football uniform at the age of twelve. He looked so goofy," Stephen said. "I mean, he had long skinny arms, braces on his teeth, and wore glasses. I could barely look at him. I was embarrassed that he was me. No wonder none of the girls would talk to me. The guys in football called me noodle arms. He was so ugly."

"What was that like for that twelve-year-old?" I questioned.

"It was terrible," said Stephen. "I used to come home from school, shut my bedroom door, and cry. Once my father saw me crying and he called me a sissy. He told me to 'buck up' and be a man. My dad was such a jerk."

"Stephen," I quietly said, "when you look at the picture of that boy with disdain and criticism, you are treating him in the same way that your peers and father treated him. You are sustaining the shame that already lies in the heart of that child and therefore in your own heart. You must not forget that he is you. You would never tell a twelve-year-old that he was goofy and ugly, would you?"

"No," replied Stephen, "I would not. It really breaks my heart to think of him being ridiculed and teased. I guess I need to take another look at that picture and maybe give him a little extra time, attention, and love."

"Yes, Stephen," I stated. "I think it is time to take care of him. He really needs you."

Seven

Reparenting the Child:

Making the Connection

The initial step in healing your childhood woundedness is to recognize and fully accept that your value comes from your very existence and that all people are precious children of an all-loving divinity. If you were raised in a religious environment that depicted a vengeful, angry God who created mankind as being essentially evil, it may be difficult to develop and believe in the concept of your birth-created value. Changing those religious childhood messages can be quite challenging. One helpful technique in changing those messages is meditating upon the beauty of nature. It would be fundamentally incongruent for a tyrannical Higher Power to create such magnificent beauty for mankind to enjoy if that Higher Power did not fully value you, his child.

Another helpful exercise is writing note cards that describe the loving nature of God. These can be scriptures, mantras, or quotes from various forms of spiritual literature. You should read the note cards several times a day so that thought changes can occur. Changing your belief system will take time and persistence, so don't become discouraged. This one fundamental change will play a significant role in the healing process.

If you do not believe in any sort of divine being, you might be able to identify with a loving energy that permeates the world. In twelve-step recovery groups, it is often suggested that those who have difficulty believing in any type of Higher Power start by believing that the group itself is a form of a Higher Power. A willingness to believe frequently results in an actual belief. Rather than it making sense cognitively, it will resonate as a truth in your soul.

Behavior and self-value must be separated.

While developing belief in your birth-created value, it's important to remind yourself constantly that your behavior, looks, and accomplishments are totally separate from your value. This is an absolutely essential component in the process of loving yourself. You may behave in ways that are atrocious and damaging to others and yet your value remains unaffected. Behavior and self-value must be separated. People who act offensively toward others are acting out of a sense of shame. In order to compensate for feelings of inadequacy, people will try to one-up others with arrogance, putdowns, gossip, judgment, and self-righteous indignation. Shame leaves people feeling disempowered, while offensive behaviors create an illusion of power over others.

Steps to Reparenting the Wounded Child

Step 1—Have Compassion for the Wounded Child

Your original childhood wounds are healed as you learn to have compassion for your own woundedness. *Encarta College Dictionary* defines compassion as "sympathy for the suffering of others, often including a desire to help." You learn to look at your child self and feel sympathy for the suffering of that child. You then tell yourself that you are helping your internal child by giving him the nurturing that was lacking during his childhood. Healing your childhood wounds can be quite emotional. If you become overwhelmed with your feelings at any time during this exercise, please contact a trained professional to guide you in the process.

At this point you may be saying, "My childhood was not that bad. There are a lot of people who had it much worse and I know that my parents did the best they could do." Clients are often very reluctant to rat out their parents. This may be especially true for you if your family system "looked really good" on the outside. Your parents may have been more covertly abusive than others. If you compare your childhood wounds to the wounds of those who experienced more overt abuse, you will minimize, rationalize, and justify your parents' behaviors. Remember that the purpose of this process is not to judge or blame your parents. It is to examine the parenting practices that were non-nurturing so that you do not continue to live life from the effects of these practices. Your parents are not bad people; they are wounded themselves. Their own personal childhood experiences were filled with insufficient nurturing, which in turn became their blueprint for parenting. In short, your parents practiced the dysfunctional parenting skills that they learned from their parents.

It's time now for you to focus on healing yourself so that you can live a fully functional adult life filled with abundance.

Doing the healing work through your inner child is key because it is easier for you as an adult to have compassion for your child self than to have compassion for your adult self. When people try to have compassion for themselves as adults, they often say, "I do not want to feel sorry for myself." If you start to feel sorry for yourself as you think about your own childhood experiences, try the following exercise:

1. Think of a child you love. This could be your own child, a niece or nephew, or the child of a friend.

2. Imagine that you are watching that child experience one or more of the painful events that you remember experiencing as a child.

3. Ask yourself if you feel sad, angry, or fearful as you watch that child having that particular experience. Write down the feelings. Ask yourself what you think that child is feeling. Is he or she feeling sad, angry, or afraid? Write down the feelings.

4. Now picture that child along with yourself as a child having that same painful experience together.

5. Do you feel the same emotions watching your child self as you did when you were watching the original

child having the same experience? What do you imagine your child self is feeling? Is he or she feeling sad, angry, or afraid? Write down the feelings.

6. If you felt the same feelings for your child self as you did for the original child in your imagination, congratulations! You have connected to the wounded child that lives deep within your soul. Imagine wrapping your arms around that precious child to comfort him or her. Hold your child self in your arms and tell your child self that you love him or her and that he or she is safe. That child is you. Feel it. Experience it. Release any sadness that arises and allow yourself to feel deep compassion for the part of yourself that you had forgotten. It is time.

7. Reconnect with your child self several times during the day. Do it first thing in the morning and before you go to sleep. You cannot reconnect with your child self too often. You will never be without your child self again; you have been away from one another for entirely too long. Oh, that precious child!

Seeing your wounded child with compassion is seeing your wounded child with the eyes of the heart. When you are able to see your own wounded child with the eyes of the heart, you will then be able to see your adult self with the eyes of the heart. At this point, you will start to become immune to the toxic effects of shame that have impeded your life and separated you from your rightful inheritance—joy, peace, and abundance.

Step 2—Create a Trauma Timeline

Creating a timeline of traumatic childhood experiences and the resulting internalized messages is the next step in the healing process. After reading the first section of *The Shame Game*, you should have a fairly good comprehension of the parenting techniques that created your shame core. You probably have also begun to identify childhood experiences and messages that you now realize were traumatic for you. These childhood experiences and messages will be placed on a timeline so that you will have a visual of your traumatic past. You will begin to understand how you are living your life based either on your reaction to the experiences or on the dos and don'ts of your childhood messages or "marching orders." Marching orders tend to be rigid, black or white, and nonnegotiable.

When you were a child, you automatically adhered to the marching orders in order to survive in the family system. You simply could not have gotten away with bucking that system. As an adult, subconsciously, those marching orders are the "rules" by which you continue to live your life. Sometimes these guidelines can be helpful and will continue to be an intrinsic part of your value system, but some of these rules are no longer beneficial to functional adulthood. As an adult, you now have a choice. You can keep what you like and throw away the rest. You cannot get a spanking. You cannot get grounded. You simply can no longer get in trouble with your parents or any other human being. There may be consequences to breaking societal rules such as speeding or stealing, but the freedom lies in having a choice.

Begin your trauma timeline by reflecting upon and then writing about the childhood shame-based events that you experienced with your parents or primary caregiver, other family members, church, school, peers, or society. This can be done in story form or by listing the shame-based events according to the source of the experience. If you choose to use a story format to freely express and remember your shame-based experiences, you should then place the events in a list according to the source of the experience. After listing the experiences, go back and write about the resulting messages that you internalized as a child as well as your age at the time of the events. The age should be based on your earliest memory regarding the event. Below is an example of the list format. The events and internalized messages that are used in the example are based on Heather's story that can be found at the beginning of chapter six.

Parental/Primary Caregiver Events and Messages

- **Event:** My father did not ever talk about his feelings.
  Message: It is not OK or important for me to talk about feelings with people.
  Age: Six

- **Event:** My father got angry with my mother because she was not happy all of the time. My mother would get mad at my sister and me when we got angry with each other.

Message: I should always be happy and so should other people.
Age: Eight

- **Event:** It was very important to my mother that she was thin and looked perfect. My mother would get angry with my sister and me if we did not look and act perfectly.
  Message: I am more lovable when I look and act perfectly. It is *very* important that I am pretty and skinny. I must do whatever it takes to be skinny. I need to exercise a lot and restrict my eating.
  Age: Ten and sixteen

- **Event:** My father would yell and spank me with a belt, and my mother would yell and spank me with a spoon.
  Message: It is all right to hit someone that I love if I do not like what they do, and it is all right for people who love me to yell at me and hit me. It is OK to yell at those whom I love.
  Age: Six and sixteen

- **Event:** My parents acted the happiest when I performed, won competitions, and made good grades. My father would come home from work to spank my sister and me when we made my mother angry.
  Message: My job is to make my parents proud and happy and not make them feel angry or sad. I am responsible for the feelings of others.
  Age: Ten

School Events and Messages

- **Event:** I was frequently the teacher's helper because I made straight As.

  Message: I am more valuable than others if I make good grades. People will like me if I make good grades. Making good grades is defined as making straight As and anything less than that is not good enough.

  Age: Eight

- **Event:** When I won spelling bees and math competitions, the principal put my name on a bulletin board and my teachers would let me be the class leader.

  Message: I am more valuable when I win competitions. It is essential that I am a high achiever.

  Age: Eight

Religious Events and Messages

- **Event:** The preacher would yell about how God hates sin and how I am a sinner because I was born that way.

  Message: If I sin, God will hate me because God hates sin and sinners are bad.

  Age: Eight

- **Event:** The preacher talked about the rage of God. He also talked about how God killed people, like when the earth was flooded, because He was angry with them.

Message: God might get angry with me sometimes. As a result, God might hurt me or cause something bad to happen to me.
Age: Seven

- **Event:** The preacher yelled that people who were not Christians were going to go to hell when they died.
Message: If I am not a real Christian, I will burn in hell and spend eternity with the devil. People who believe differently from me are going to Hell when they die.
Age: Nine

- **Event:** The preacher, Sunday school teachers, and my parents talked about how important it was to be a good Christian and go to church every Sunday, go to Sunday school, sing in the choir, and attend all church affairs.
Message: To be a "good Christian," I should attend church every time the door is open. There is the possibility that I can be a bad person.
Age: Nine

- **Event:** The preacher yelled that God hates divorce and therefore divorce is never permissible.
Message: If someone gets a divorce, God will be angry with him or her. I can never get a divorce, no matter what happens in my marriage.
Age: Sixteen

- **Event:** The preacher yelled that homosexuality was a sin.

  Message: God does not love homosexuals. Homosexuals are bad people.

  Age: Sixteen

Social Events and Messages

- **Event:** My friends teased me about my freckles and crooked teeth.

  Message: I am not lovable if I have any physical flaws.

  Age: Ten

- **Event:** After having braces on my teeth, the boys liked me. The boys were mean to the girls who were not thin.

  Message: If I am skinny and attractive, I am more lovable.

  Age: Fifteen

- **Event:** When I had my first boyfriend, I felt happier than I had ever felt before.

  Message: When I have a boyfriend, I am truly happy. Having a boyfriend makes me feel lovable.

  Age: Fifteen

- **Event:** My boyfriend yelled at me and cheated on me. He said that it was because I had been a bitch.

> **Message:** It is important for me to be the perfect girlfriend and forgive my boyfriend so that he does not go away.
>
> **Age:** Sixteen

- **Event:** I drank alcohol with my friends as a way to medicate the shame that I felt and as a way to rebel against my controlling parents.

  Message: When I feel shame, pain, or anger, I need to medicate those feelings.

  Age: Sixteen

Although this is a fairly time-consuming and extensive process, it is extremely important to get a clear picture of your childhood marching orders. Once you have clarified the messages that you automatically internalized as a child, you can then discard the shame-based messages that continue to sustain behaviors and beliefs that no longer are effective for you as an adult.

Make a list of the shame-based messages that no longer work for you as an adult and have a ceremonial release of these messages.

Examples:

- Tie the messages to a balloon and release them to your Higher Power.
- Burn the messages and visualize the messages turning into smoke.
- Bury the messages in your backyard and consider them no longer.

Step 3—Reconnect with the Child through Photo Visualization

Now that you have created a childhood timeline, you are ready to connect visually with the inner child. This is done most effectively by using your childhood photographs. If possible, the photos should correspond to the ages of the shame messages you recalled in the timeline. Because these occurrences were at various stages of development, it is important to find photos that are age appropriate to those messages.

The healing process will actually release the frozen feelings of the child that you have carried with you into adulthood.

Once you have the photos, your objective is to reconnect with the child by having compassion for him. In my experience, the easiest way to accomplish that is by looking into the child's eyes. By doing so, you can reflect on how the child felt while he was having that experience. As you look at your childhood photographs, you may be flooded with emotions such as sadness or anger. This is to be expected. Because you were unable to fully feel and express your childhood feelings, the feelings were repressed and frozen deep within your subconscious. The healing process will actually release the frozen feelings of the child that you have carried with you into adulthood. Do not resist these feelings as they emerge. If you feel sad, cry. If you feel angry, hit a pillow or stomp around the room. If you feel fear or anxiety, breathe deeply and then blow out the fear. By feeling your feelings, you are cleansing your subconscious and honoring yourself as a child.

When you visit that child in photos, it is crucial to talk to the child as a loving and nurturing parent. In those conversations, you should speak with compassion and tell the child what he needed to hear in his youth. Some nurturing examples are as follows:

- I understand how painful that experience must have been for you. I understand why you would feel shame, anger, fear, or sadness.
- You are precious.
- You are valuable.
- I love you.
- You are safe.
- I am going to take care of you.
- It has taken me a long time to be here with you, but I am here now. I will never leave you again.

Doing this while looking at the eyes of the child allows you to see the preciousness and woundedness in the child's eyes. Understanding your childhood pain is an important part of healing. Once you can look at the child with tenderness and compassion, you can then begin to shift that awareness to yourself. Remember, you are that child.

When I did this work myself, I carried a picture of myself at age eight in my wallet for two years. This was my age when I internalized the message that it was my job to be the emotional caretaker of others. When I talk about this with my clients, I laugh and say that although I still have the job of helping others learn to take care of themselves emotionally, I finally decided to get paid for it. It is not a negative thing to care about others, but an "emotional caretaker" will take care of others at their own expense. Emotional caretakers feel responsible for making others happy, proud, and lovable, while disregarding their own feelings. Every time I took money from my wallet, I looked into the eight-year-old's eyes and pictured telling her that she was precious and that I loved her. I continue to keep a picture of myself at age nine by my makeup mirror. Each morning I look in that little girl's eyes and tell her how precious she is. Then I look into my own eyes and tell myself how precious I am. This practice continues to keep me aware of my value and has kindled a love for my little girl self that is equivalent to the love I have for my own children and grandchildren. You, too, will learn to love and adore your little child self.

This process should be repeated frequently. It can be done while you are getting ready in the morning, washing your hands, at work, or before you go to bed at night. Carry a picture of yourself as a child in your wallet or purse. Tape a picture to the bathroom mirror, stick one on the refrigerator, and place one by your bedside. Take a picture to work with you or carry one in your pocket. Remind this child of his preciousness daily. Look into the child's eyes, see his value, and feel his preciousness. Now look into your own eyes in the mirror. Recognize and feel that same value. As you look into the mirror, you will see the soul of the child that is within you. Tell your adult self that you, too, are precious and valuable.

Chapter Seven Exercises:
What You Can Do

S ince this chapter is laid out as an exercise in itself, take time to go through each step at your own pace and work through the activities. Be prepared—this process can be emotionally challenging and exhausting, but it is so worth it. And it works.

Steps to Reparenting the Wounded Child:
- **Step 1**—Have compassion for the wounded child
- **Step 2**—Create a trauma timeline
- **Step 3**—Reconnect with the child through photo visualization

Eight

"*Ever'thing there is but lovin'
leaves a rust on yo' soul.*"

—Langston Hughes—

After having a series of failed relationships and working ridiculously long hours at a prestigious law firm, Kristan came to see me because she was ready to make some changes in her life. She wanted to be in a loving, committed relationship and she wanted to start a private law practice. There was only one problem—Kristan was scared to death. Although she wanted change, Kristan had absolutely no faith in her ability to achieve the desires of her heart. You guessed it—Kristan was filled with shame.

I spent the first couple of sessions with Kristan learning about her family system and teaching her about shame. She readily wrapped her brain around all of the concepts and understood how toxic shame and the resulting shame core were sabotaging her life. In our previous session, we talked about the importance of connecting with herself as a child, and she began the connecting process. Kristan was ready to fix the problem.

"OK, Janice," Kristan said impatiently. "I have connected with those little girls and I am trying to love them.

I do realize that I have been living my life from shame and as a wounded little girl. It is really unbelievable how powerful those marching orders are and how much they have affected my choices and my life. But I am sick of those brats running amok. It really annoys me. I want to live my life in a way that is adult so that I can be happy. What on earth am I supposed to do with those little girls now? I mean, really. I am thirty-two years old. It's time to get them out of here so we can get this show on the road."

"Calm down a little bit, Kristan," I advised. "I know you are anxious to be 'fixed,' but we don't want to chop their little heads off. Remember, they have only done what they were taught to do. Your job now is to love them and treat them with compassion. Once they feel safe and truly believe that you have their back, they will lose their voice and stop interfering in your life. They will learn to silently rest in your heart and joyfully watch as you live in abundance."

"I get it," laughed Kristan. "I guess I am being a little harsh. Just tell me what to do and I will do it. Actually this is pretty good practice as to how Mr. Wonderful and I will love our own children."

"Exactly," I said. "Let's get started."

Eight

Reparenting the Child

Loving What Is

After you have connected with the child within, you are ready to reparent. Reparenting is the process in which you give your inner child what he needed to receive from his primary caregivers but did not, such as the realization of his created value. This is an important process because as an adult you can never experience true joy and abundant living without first realizing your value. As we have already established, the shame-filled child becomes an adult with alternate forms of self-esteem and addiction issues. Without reparenting the child, you will not experience true self-esteem and will not be able to sustain a life free from shame-based dysfunctional issues and behaviors.

Step 1—Reparenting the Child through Visualization

Take out the pictures that you have previously assembled as part of your timeline. As you look into the eyes of yourself as a child, you will reparent that child by doing the following:

1. Validate the child's reality. Look at each individual picture. Give each child a voice by asking them what they want to say. In other words, if the child in the picture could speak, what would he say about his shame-based childhood experiences and internalized shame messages? Then say to the child, "I understand why you think, behave, and feel that way. By doing so, you were able to survive and I thank you for that."

2. Nurture the child. Look at each picture and say, "I love you. You are precious. You are valuable. You are safe." Each of these statements is essential in order for the child to feel nurtured.

3. Set limits for the child. Look at each picture and say, "I cannot let you live my life for me now by continuing to think, behave, and feel that way. I can no longer allow you to determine my value. I am going to live my life from an adult place full of self-esteem. I am going to take care of you now."

4. Tell each child that you are going to place them into your heart where you will lovingly parent them and keep them safe. Hold out your right hand with the palm facing upward. Visualize each child sitting in the palm of your hand. Now place each child into your heart, where they will live and be protected.

5. Sit for a couple of minutes with your eyes closed and picture the children resting peacefully in your heart. Gently pat your chest above your heart and tell the children that they are safe and that you love them. Picture the children feeling loved and relieved that you have finally removed them from having to live your life for you. It is exhausting to be a grown-up on the outside and let a child rule your world.

By completing this process, you should begin to feel peaceful. You have lovingly stopped the children from attempting to live your adult life. Their survival techniques are no longer needed and they are finally safe. They can remain as a part of your spirit without creating havoc in your world. They are exactly where they are supposed to be.

Writing the Child a Letter

Another exercise to heal the child within is writing the child a letter. A letter is the perfect opportunity to give the child the healthy messages that they needed to receive from caregivers, religious teachers, schoolteachers, peers, or society. Here is an example of a childhood letter that is based on Heather's story:

My Dear Little Heather,

You are so very precious and I love you very much. There were some things that happened to you that were damaging and hurtful, and I feel very sad that you experienced these things. As a little girl, you could not have known that the big people in your life were wrong to hurt you as they did, but now I am going to tell you the truth about how wonderful you are.

Your feelings are a very important part of who you are and you should have never been made to feel shame about feeling sad or angry. Your preciousness and value have nothing to do with how you look, what kind of grades you make, or how well you perform a particular task. It is never OK for someone to hit you or yell at you, and you deserve to be treated kindly by everyone. Although it is important that you treat others kindly, you are never responsible for other people's feelings. Other people can take care of themselves and deal with their own feelings.

It was absolutely terrible that you were told that God might be unhappy with you for doing something wrong. God loves you no matter what you do and that can never change. God loves you unconditionally and thinks that you are fantastic! God would never hurt you or anyone else even if they believe differently from you or you believe differently from them.

You should have been told that your value could never change and that having a boyfriend does not give you more value than you already have. Boys should treat you with kindness and should never cheat on you. If a boy does cheat on you, walk away from him. Even though you might feel sad about not being with the boy, you deserve to be with someone who is honest and faithful. There is no need to medicate feelings even if others choose to do so, and you should have been told to care for yourself with loving tenderness.

I feel really sad that you were not nurtured to realize your value. It was wrong. But I am going to take care of you now and I am going to tell you every day how spectacular you are. You are tremendously valuable simply because you breathe the air. I love you.

—Adult Heather

Step 2—Healing the Abuse

Healing childhood abuse takes time. You as an adult will heal your childhood abuse primarily through feeling compassion and love for your abused child self. This is not wallowing in self-pity; it is remembering how it felt for you as a child. Drawing a picture from the child's perspective and writing a letter to the person who was abusive to you are ways to help heal from abusive childhood experiences.

The Drawing Process:

1. Place a piece of drawing paper in front of you.

2. Shut your eyes and try to remember the child (you) at the earliest age of abuse. Try to connect with the child as you imagine him feeling shame, sadness, anger, or fear.

3. Open your eyes and now try to recreate those feelings by using your nondominant hand to draw a picture of what the child was feeling and experiencing.

4. Don't worry about how your drawing looks. It may be a picture, markings, or even scribbles.

5. As feelings arise, feel them and release them. It is normal to feel sad or angry.

6. Hang the picture where you can see it for a period of time, at least a couple of weeks. If possible, tape a picture of yourself at the time of the abuse somewhere close to the picture. Connect with the child whenever you look at the picture and tell the child that he or she is safe.

The Letter-Writing Process:

We do not heal our own abuse by abusing our abusers.

This letter should be written to the person or people who were responsible for inflicting the spiritual, emotional, sexual, intellectual, physical, or verbal abuse. Write what you would say to the abuser if you felt emotionally and physically safe enough to say whatever you wanted. Do not try to assuage the abuser's feelings by feeling guilty for saying something that you think would hurt him or her. Although you may choose to mail the letter at a later date, do not do so immediately. Allow some healing time to pass. Most of the time, people choose not to mail the letter because they don't feel that it would help them heal. Remember, this process is for your own healing rather than needing to make a point with someone else. We do not heal our own abuse by abusing our abusers.

The following is a sample letter that was written by a client who was sexually abused by her brother. The client agreed to have her letter included in this book. Identifying details and names have been changed in order to protect the individuals involved.

Dear Ted,

You made me feel like the coolest kid. I had an older brother who would hang out with me, take me out with him and his friends, protect me, and make me feel safe. You took me horseback riding with William. You let me stay out late with you and Terry in the backyard, making forts in the tree house. You took me out to a bar.

You took me to the lake with your friends. You taught me how to smoke in high school. We had a special relationship. I remember when you were always in trouble, and I told you one day that I loved you. You looked at me as if no one had said that to you, and truly meant it, in years. You told me how much that meant to you. It was great. We supported each other in a way that no one else did.

But you took advantage of me. It wasn't your place to teach me everything. You had no right to make me feel your penis. I trusted you. I looked up to you. I thought you were the coolest older brother. I thought that I was in on this secret that no one else knew. You used that power to make me feel small and weak. I felt motionless.

I didn't want to lose what we had, but I knew it was wrong. It felt wrong. It felt gross. I didn't want you to not like me anymore. I wanted to protect you. I wanted to believe that you were the great older brother. I wanted others to see that you weren't always the bad kid in the family.

I was never angry with you, just confused and scared. But how could you do that? You protected me from everyone else. I trusted you and you take advantage of me? I'm still scared of what would happen if I told you or the family about this.

That's the part that pisses me off the most—that I am too scared of making waves to stand up for myself, for my rights. If this happened to our nieces, I would be screaming, but not for myself. Why can't I scream for myself? You wronged me and I did/have done nothing about it. This was not my fault. It was your decision. It was yours. Why do I take ownership over what happened to me? Is it more important for people to like me than to protect myself?

I have such mixed emotions about you. I hate that you took advantage of me, but I love the love you gave me. You can get so angry and filled with rage that I don't want to set you off. I don't want to bring up something that will make you angry. But does that mean that I should have to live with this? Should I suffer simply because I don't want you to get angry?

Ted, that was f——ed up. It was wrong. How dare you treat me like that? You disrespected me, you hurt me, and you made me fearful of you. I was a sweet, nice, funny, innocent, sheltered little girl. I loved everyone. I tried to make everyone happy and you sexualized me. You made me feel wrong and dirty and like this was something that I had to carry. I don't care what you were going through. That was not something I should ever have had to deal with. Screw you for putting me there. For making me feel tiny. For making me protect you. For making me choose you over me.

So from here on out, I'm absolving myself from allowing others' feelings to take precedence over mine. This is your problem, not mine.

—Susan

Drawing a picture from the child's perspective and writing a letter may release some intense and seemingly overwhelming feelings. When children experience abuse, they will frequently freeze their pain, fear, anger, and shame. This is a defense mechanism that the child will employ in order to help him or her survive and cope with the abuse. Because the abuser is not honoring the child's reality, the child will detach from what is happening to him, freeze the feelings, and focus on getting through the abuse.

As you use these healing techniques to reconnect with yourself as a wounded child, the child's reality is finally being acknowledged. This acknowledgment will thaw the frozen feelings and they will surface. Although you might tend to resist the frozen childhood feelings, the feelings need to be released in order to be cleared. What you feel you can begin to heal. Even though feelings are not facts, they are an important part of who we are. The feelings that we resist and either partially feel or totally censor will persist. Fear that is resisted turns into anxiety. Anxiety that is resisted turns into panic. Sadness that is resisted turns into depression or anxiety. Anger that is resisted turns into depression, anxiety, or rage.

The following method is an effective way to release feelings:

1. Shut your eyes and breathe deeply.

2. Identify the feelings by saying to yourself, "I am feeling sadness, anger, fear, guilt, or shame."

3. Release the feelings with appropriate action. Release sadness by crying. Release fear by breathing in the fear and then blowing it out. Release anger by hitting a pillow, stomping around a room, or yelling about your anger in privacy.

4. Allow yourself to sit in the feeling for a sustained period of time. I typically advise sitting in a feeling for up to ten minutes. It is sometimes helpful to set a timer so that you sit long enough to experience a cleansing effect.

5. After you feel the repressed feelings for the designated time period, do something loving and nurturing for yourself. A warm bath, a massage, or a walk outside may feel nurturing. If you have expressed a lot of sadness, you may feel extremely exhausted. If this is the case, take a nap or lie down for a rest.

6. Repeat the above feeling method as often as needed. This method can be used whenever you are experiencing uncomfortable feelings.

7. If you have difficulty connecting with your sadness because you were taught that feeling sadness was unacceptable, watch a movie that has caused you sadness in the past. This sometimes helps thaw and release the frozen sadness from childhood.

I have heard clients say that they are hesitant to feel their feelings because they are afraid that the feelings will never cease. Sadness, in particular, is uncomfortable to feel. Rest assured, you will eventually get to the bottom of the frozen feelings and they will not return. You will not cry the same tears again once they are expressed. There may be more behind those released, but the sadness will end. Make noise with your sadness—open your mouth and don't forget to breathe. As you grieve your childhood experience and release your inner child's unfelt feelings, you will feel relief. Although the grief process is exhausting, it clears the way for joy. Remember, what you *feel* can be *healed*.

Step 3—Acceptance

Acceptance means that you can live your life free from the past, free from the abuse, free from the effects of the abuse, and free from the abuser.

The last step in the healing process is acceptance. Acceptance does not mean that what you experienced as a child was OK. It was not OK. It will never be OK for children, including yourself, to experience shame and abuse.

As you reflect on your childhood experiences, you will always feel compassion and sadness for that child. You will always feel anger toward the abuser, but the anger will be reasonable and will not fill you with rage. Acceptance does not eliminate adult feelings. Acceptance simply means that what you experienced as a child is what you experienced. It was what it was. Acceptance means that you can live your life free from the past, free from the abuse, free from the effects of the abuse, and free from the abuser.

Because you have begun to feel your childhood feelings, connected with that precious child, and started reparenting that lovable, wounded child, you are no longer bound to the events and internalized messages from your childhood. They no longer unknowingly own you and control your experiences, thoughts, feelings, and behaviors. You are now ready to begin to live life as an adult. You are now ready to begin to live a life that is happy, joyous, and free. You are now ready to begin to live your life from choice, a life filled with love for self and others. You can now recognize your birth-created value and you are beginning to experience true self-esteem. You are ready to begin to live life *abundantly*. Enjoy!

Chapter Eight Exercises:
What You Can Do

L ike chapter seven, this chapter is laid out with various activities for you to practice as you work through the material. Absorb the ideas and pick what works for you at this time. Revisit the content as necessary and expand your repertoire of tools to reparent your inner child.

- **Step 1**—Reparenting the child through visualization
  Writing the child a letter
- **Step 2**—Healing the abuse
  The drawing process
  The letter-writing process
- **Step 3**—Acceptance

Although the practice of healing is a process rather than an event, you have started down the road to wholeness. Every time you repeat one of the above-mentioned processes, you will realize a new part of your childhood experience that needs to be mended. Uncovering the layers of trauma that yearn for discovery and healing is like peeling an onion.

IV

Doing the Work:
Mental Boot Camp

Nine

"The Universe is run exactly on the lines of a cafeteria. Unless you claim—mentally—what you want, you may sit and wait forever."

—Emmet Fox—

*M*any years ago, there was an innocent man who was arrested by a baron. The man was thrown into the baron's dark and clammy dungeon, and the large metal door to the dungeon was slammed shut. A huge, burly guard was ordered to stand outside the dungeon door and was instructed not to talk to the man at all.

The man was devastated at the thought of being away from his family and friends. "How could I be so unlucky?" thought the man. "I have done nothing to deserve this sort of treatment. I have paid my rent on time and I am always looking for someone to help. There are plenty of people who do wrong unto others. They should be here instead of me. How could life be so unfair?" Day after day, night after night, the man ruminated about the disservice that life had bestowed upon him. He felt like a victim and dreamed of getting even with the baron.

After remaining in the dungeon for twenty years, living on bread and water and without any correspondence from friends *and family, the man decided that he could no longer stand being imprisoned. He wanted to die. He devised a plan to attack the guard when the guard brought the man his daily bread and water, knowing that the guard would kill him.*

For the first time since his imprisonment, the man examined the door. The door was unlocked! "How can this be?" thought the man. "The guard must have forgotten to lock the door last night when he left me my bread and water. This will be easy. I am sure that the guard will kill me the moment I open the door." Although the man was fearful of dying, he believed that his death would be better than living in this terrible place.

It took all the man's strength to push open the door, but he finally got it open wide enough to leave. He took a deep breath. As the man exited the dungeon, he looked at the guard and prepared himself for the blow that would surely take his life. Nothing happened. The guard simply stared straight ahead and did not move a muscle. The man walked past the guard without receiving any reaction from the guard whatsoever.

The man continued to walk through the baron's castle, past soldiers and guards, and no one paid any attention to him. They acted as if he did not exist. No one chased the man and no one yelled at him to stop. As he left the castle, the man walked over the drawbridge and past the bridge guard. He looked over his shoulder, fully expecting to see soldiers chasing after him, but he saw no one. At last, after twenty years of imprisonment, the man was free!

You see, the man was not a prisoner of people, mortar, steel, or stone, but rather the man had spent twenty years as a prisoner of his false belief!

Nine

Unlocking the Possibilities:

You Hold the Keys

If you have been living with a toxic shame core, you have been unable to live your life in the fullness of abundance. On a deep level, you have believed that you were unworthy of a rich and fulfilling life. Toxic shame has become a barrier that stifles the flow of prosperous living. Prosperity, in all areas of your life, is yours for the taking once you are mentally and emotionally prepared. As you learn to see your own preciousness, self-esteem pours out, accompanied by joy and love. Living with self-esteem allows you to recognize not only the value in yourself but also the value in others. Self-esteem releases you from destructive thoughts and behaviors toward yourself and others.

Once you recognize your value, your esteem tank becomes full and you can begin to rightfully pursue your own good intentions. Your good intentions are based solely on your wants, rather than on your needs. No longer will your pursuits be about replacing shame with a need, but you will be working to realize your true heart's wants and desires. Your higher self will now seek purpose through adequate self-esteem, and in doing so you will pursue healthy intentions.

The following represent some common healthy intentions that you may choose to incorporate into your life.

Healthy Relationships

A healthy relationship is one based on desire rather than need.

A healthy relationship is one based on desire rather than need. In a healthy relationship, you will not lose yourself nor will you insist that your partner lose himself or herself. As a matter of fact, you would not want your partner to lose himself or herself, because you honor the very essence of your partner as being precious. In a healthy relationship, no one is too needy and neither person is needless or want-less. Both extremes are toxic shame responses and will not be palatable for individuals who recognize their own intrinsic value.

As partners, you will feel safe and you will be committed to the spiritual development of both individuals. You will be real and vulnerable because there is no need to act like a chameleon to please your partner, and you will understand that each of you is different as opposed to being "right" or "wrong."

You will say what you mean, mean what you say, and will not be mean when you say it. You will be able to agree to disagree and you will be able to resolve conflict without extreme volatility. Your life together will be a place of commitment and kindness, resulting in connection as well as personal growth.

I believe that it is very important to be able to be happy with yourself, away from a significant other relationship, before you will be able to find an abundant relationship. When I got divorced at age forty-two, I had *never* been without a boyfriend for more than a couple of months. As a result, I was miserable and terrified of being alone. I had to learn to love being with myself.

Every Friday night when my kids were busy with their activities and were away from our house, I had a date night with myself. Sometimes I put on my favorite robe, ate popcorn and frozen yogurt, and watched a really good movie. Other times I put on my favorite music and looked at magazines. I would get a fashion magazine, a travel magazine, a home decorating magazine, and a food magazine. When I saw a picture of something that I really liked or a picture of how I wanted my new life to unfold, I tore out the pictures and started a "Janice" file.

Because I had never before spent time really getting to know myself the way I did during that first year out of my marriage, I learned a lot about myself. I think back on those nights with warmth in my heart, as I literally became my own BFF (best friend forever)!

Financial Security

Financial security represents the ebb and flow of money, void of fear and panic. You may have had money messages in childhood that were based on fear, creating a deep feeling of financial insecurity that you have taken into adulthood. The fear of financial insecurity can be paralyzing even when you have money in the bank. If your esteem is based on money or what money can provide, any dip in your financial status will cause you a great deal of angst. As a result of healing your toxic shame, however, your financial fears will tend to dissipate.

You now recognize your rightful place in the universe and you learn to trust in the Universe's ability to provide *through* you. As an adult with self-esteem, you will place an appropriate value on money, realizing that your wants and needs are met in perfect timing. You will not spend money that you do not have, and you will not hoard your money for fear of running out. You no longer need to buy things to "look" valuable, and you can buy things without having buyer's remorse because you believe that you deserve both pleasures and necessities. You will understand that the river of abundance runs through the universe and there is plenty to go around. Money becomes a medium of exchange rather than a badge of honor that represents your value to the world.

Physical Health

Physical health is an important element in living abundantly. When you feel healthy and your body is free from aches, pain, and disease, you have more energy and it is easier for your outlook on life to be more positive. Because abundant living begins and ends with your thinking, it is vitally important that you love yourself enough to take care of that precious body of yours. You must tell yourself that you are a healthy, vibrant human being and that your body can and will maintain a state of well-being.

In order to sustain a healthy body, it is important to practice healthy eating habits, exercise regularly, receive adequate sleep, and set aside time for relaxation and downtime. Before I learned to love and value myself, I pushed myself to do things even when I was not feeling well. I rarely got enough sleep, I overexercised, and I was literally unable to sit still and do "nothing." My body responded to this overactivity with migraine headaches and spastic colon, and I was always tired.

As I learned to live from a place of self-esteem, my headaches and stomach issues disappeared and my energy level soared. Taking care of yourself physically is one of the most important things you can do in your pursuit of abundance!

Satisfying Career Pursuits

Doing work that you enjoy, earning pay that is satisfying, and seeking your passion are key elements in enjoying abundant career success. Many people work at a job they despise, greeting the dreaded Monday morning with loathing and despair.

You absolutely cannot live in abundance unless you really like what you do as a career.

If you hate your job, find a new one. You absolutely cannot live in abundance unless you really like what you do as a career. You must seek your passion in your work. When you do so, you will meet the day with joy as opposed to dread. You should feel about your job the same way you feel about your sport. You may not want to do your job twenty-four hours a day, seven days a week, but you will start your day with joy and end your day with satisfaction. Find a job or career that gets your internal juices flowing and you will be financially satisfied. You will be healthier physically and you will be happier. People will want to be around you because you smile more readily and seem more pleasant and relaxed.

If you need to go back to school, then do so. Even if you have to attend school or a job-training course on a part-time basis, you will accomplish your goal eventually. I thought about going to graduate school at age forty-two, but I kept thinking that it was too late. I told a friend that I wanted to go to school but was hesitant because I would be forty-five by the time I finished. My friend wisely told me that I would be forty-five in three years anyway—with or without my postgraduate degree. Duh! I enrolled in graduate school, got my master's degree, and now have a very successful and fulfilling psychotherapy practice. Thank God for my friend!

Emotional and Mental Health

Learning to take care of yourself emotionally and mentally are vital factors in obtaining abundance—life lessons very few of us learned as children. In many cases, our role models had no such practice, and we often watched our caregivers suffer from depression, anxiety, or other forms of mental illness.

If you grew up with parents who believed that it was your job to take care of them emotionally, then you were not taught the importance of self-care and really knowing yourself. You were taught to deny and detach from yourself—what you want, what you need, what you think, and what you feel. You were conditioned to become *hypersensitive* to the wants, needs, feelings, and thoughts of others and *hyposensitive* to your own wants, needs, feelings, and thoughts. You may have actually been told that you should die unto yourself and that it is wrong to be selfish. You were taught that it is admirable to be selfless.

Rather than viewing selfishness and selflessness as an "either/or" concept, I suggest that you view the concept in terms of a continuum. The following graph can help explain this idea.

Adult emotional maturity is found anywhere between the two outside vertical markings. I call this the "cradle of moderation" because it is where you will experience the gentle, rocking motion of practicing self-care. At times you may choose to act more on the selfish end of the continuum, while at other times you may choose to act more on the selfless end of the continuum.

When I first began my career, my children were still living at home. I was a single working mom and I was frequently exhausted after a long day of school and work. At times one of my children would call me at work and ask me to go by their favorite restaurant and pick up dinner. Sometimes I would say "yes" even though I really wanted to say "no." That was when I was choosing to act more on the selfless end of the continuum. But sometimes I would say, "No. You will just have to eat something that we already have in the kitchen." That was when I was choosing to act more on the selfish end of the continuum. Both actions are considered self-care, because I was actively making a choice rather than thinking that I should or shouldn't do one or the other.

If you have been taught to be selfless, and now you try living under the umbrella of self-care, you will often make choices about which you feel guilty. The "shame-based you" would have made a much more selfless choice. The guilt you experience is false guilt, and you need to learn to throw it away. If a client tells me that they are feeling guilty about taking care of themselves, then I respond, "Wooooo hoooo! You are doing it right!"

Meditation, breathing exercises, massage therapy, psychotherapy, and support groups are other ways through which you can learn to thrive mentally and emotionally. Not only will this "thriving" benefit you; your children will also learn the importance of total self-care as they observe you in your practice.

Meditation

Meditation is a very effective way to nurture yourself emotionally. The purpose of meditation is to quiet your busy mind and go from a state of suffering or unrest to a state of joy and bliss. In meditation you learn to leave the activity of the outside world and enter an internal world of calm. As your mind ceases to obsess, it is unable to take off on a journey of anxiety, worry, and depression. It is no longer living in the past or anticipating the future. It is in the now, which in reality is the only moment that exists. When you live in the now, you are better able to reconnect with your intuition and spiritual self.

Every individual is born with an intuitive self that can serve as an internal guidance system throughout life. As children, however, we are often taught to overthink life situations rather than to trust what our intuitive nature is telling us. For example, a young child will naturally recoil from a stranger who enters into his physical space or attempts to engage the child in any form of familiarity. If your parent honored your timidity with the stranger and commended you for not engaging with the stranger, you learned to trust your intuition. On the other hand, if your parent forced you to be "nice" and engage the stranger, or if you were reprimanded for your withdrawal, you learned to discount your intuition and ultimately denied it altogether.

This proved to be a great disservice to you as you meandered your way through adolescence and into adulthood. You were given marching orders and rules that set the standard for your responses and reactions to life. The intuitive part of your nature was silenced and was replaced with a chattering mind and restless thoughts. This becomes the seat of worry, angst, and fear. By meditating and learning to live in the now, you will be able to reconnect with your intuition and spiritual self, the seat of abundance.

If you are unaccustomed to a meditation practice, you may be intimidated by the very thought of meditating. You may find yourself saying, "There is no way I can meditate. I have trouble sitting still, much less learning to concentrate long enough to actually meditate." In actuality, meditation is an easy skill to develop once you understand that it is acquired one minute at a time. Meditation is a practice that builds upon itself, so it is important to begin slowly. Rather than criticizing yourself for doing it imperfectly, commend yourself for simply doing it. In a very short period of time, you will notice the slowing of your thoughts, and you will gain an increased awareness of the world around you. The moment you begin a meditation practice, you have entered into abundance!

There are various categories of meditation. The two we're going to concentrate on in this section are concentrative meditation, which focuses attention on breathing, chanting, or imaging, and mindfulness meditation, which focuses on an awareness of what is occurring in your world.

Concentrative Meditation:

Breathing Meditation—Breathing meditation centers on the breath and develops your ability to discipline the mind.

1. Enter a quiet room and sit in a chair with your feet flat on the floor.

2. Close your eyes and take a deep, cleansing breath through your nose. Exhale all of the breath through your mouth. Repeat.

3. With your eyes closed, begin to breathe in and out through your nose. The breaths should be at your natural pace of breathing.

4. As you breathe, silently count your breaths. Count up to ten breaths and then count backward to zero.

5. Continue this process for two minutes or longer. Setting a timer for the desired amount of time is recommended.

6. Be aware of your body sensations as air enters your nose and then as the air leaves through your nose.

Do not be alarmed if your mind wanders during this process. It is what your brain is conditioned to do. Simply return your mind to your breathing and counting. If you lose count because of your wandering mind, begin again at one. Remember, you cannot do this wrong.

Chanting—Chanting is a form of concentrative meditation that focuses on a sound or mantra. It causes your mind to center on a specific thought.

1. Enter a quiet room and sit in a chair with your feet flat on the floor.

2. Close your eyes and take a deep, cleansing breath through your nose. Exhale all of the breath through your mouth. Repeat.

3. Breathe in through your nose and as you exhale, recite a calming word or positive mantra. Although it is recommended that the word or mantra be

repeated audibly, it can also be done silently. Some examples of healing mantras are: "Let go and let God," "I deserve to experience divine abundance," "I am precious," and "I am love."

4. Repeat the word or mantra as you exhale each breath. Continue for ten minutes or more.

Imaging—Focusing on a particular image is another form of concentrative meditation and can be done with your eyes open or closed.

1. Enter a quiet room and sit in a chair with your feet flat on the floor.

2. Close your eyes and take a deep, cleansing breath through your nose. Exhale all of the breath through your mouth. Repeat.

3. Focus your mind on a pleasing mental image or open your eyes and focus on a pleasing image in your environment.

4. Hold this image in your mind or vision as you concentrate on the aspects of the image. What is its shape? Notice the richness of colors. Does it move?

5. Continue a natural rhythm of breathing as you hold the image in you mind or vision for five minutes or longer.

As stated earlier, do not become frustrated with yourself if you lose your concentration. Simply bring your mind back to the image and begin to concentrate on the image once again.

Mindfulness Meditation:

Sitting in Silence—This form of meditation develops your ability to be aware of your senses.

1. Sit in a quiet room or in a quiet place outside.
2. Close your eyes and take a deep, cleansing breath through your nose. Exhale all of the breath through your mouth. Repeat.
3. Listen to the sounds that are in your world. Can you hear birds or the leaves rustling in the wind? Take note of all of your senses. What do you see? Notice the vibrant colors and textures in nature. What do you smell? Is there a taste in your mouth? Notice how the fabric of your clothing feels against your skin. Is it soft, itchy, tight?
4. Continue to sit in this place of awareness for ten minutes or longer.

Activity Awareness—Activity awareness creates an awareness of your actions from a sensory perspective as well as developing an awareness of thoughts. In this form of meditation, you are learning to witness your world, body, and thoughts without reaction or judgment.

1. Close your eyes and take a deep, cleansing breath through your nose. Exhale all of the breath through your mouth. Repeat.
2. Open your eyes, and as you begin an activity, notice all aspects of that experience. If you are washing dishes, notice how the water feels on your hands. What is the temperature of the water? Notice the sounds that the water makes as it splashes against the sink. Can you smell the dishwashing soap? What

are your thoughts as you clean the plates? What are you feeling? Remember not to ascribe judgment to anything that you notice. You are developing an awareness of what is, not what should be or could be.

3. This technique can also be applied as a walking meditation. Notice how the ground feels under your feet. Notice the different muscles in your feet and legs as you take each step. Do your hands and arms move as you walk? Are you breathing more rapidly? Yoga is also a valuable way to practice mindfulness and awareness of your body.

As meditation is practiced, you will not only be able to increase the duration of your sessions, but you will also learn to value this gift that you are giving to yourself. You will enjoy feeling refreshed and calm as you reconnect with your self and your world.

I love this story told to me by one of my friends: On a trip to Bali, my friend asked an elderly monk what the best way to meditate was. The monk thought for a moment and then quietly said, "Go sit on a rock and keep saying to yourself, 'God, I am open to you. Please come and rest on my heart.'"

Breathing Exercises

The breath is the very essence of life and can have a healing effect on your body. Deep breathing can be used to slow your racing brain, increase your energy level, and strengthen your intestinal and abdominal muscles. It can also greatly reduce anxiety and stress.

Stress often leads to short, shallow breathing, which can contribute to physical illnesses such as high blood pressure, dizziness, and low energy. Lengthening your breath nourishes your body with oxygen, reduces toxins in your lungs, and promotes relaxation. Deep breathing also causes endorphins to be released in the brain, which helps relieve minor ailments such as headaches, backaches, sleeplessness, and other stress-related aches. Here are some tips that will help you practice deep breathing:

- Sit or lie in a comfortable position.
- Breathe deeply in through the nose for a count of six.
- As you breathe in, push out with your abdominal muscles.
- Hold your breath for another count of six.
- Now slowly release the breath from your lungs out of your mouth for a count of eight.
- As you exhale, pull in your abdominal muscles.
- Repeat this process several times.

You should begin to feel yourself relax and your heart rate lower. This is an extremely effective way to release fear or anxiety. These exercises are simple and easy to do considering that you are always breathing.

Massage Therapy

Massage therapy, the practice of manipulating the body's soft tissues and muscles, has been used as a form of healing for thousands of years. Massage is frequently viewed as a luxury; however, it has many therapeutic benefits. It can promote stress reduction and relaxation, lower blood pressure, reduce fatigue, and increase circulation and energy. Massages can increase flexibility, promote faster healing, and improve skin quality. Do yourself a giant favor and schedule a massage. You deserve this amazing treat.

Individual or Group Psychotherapy

Psychotherapy has undergone tremendous changes over the past twenty-five years and is now more accepted in our culture than ever before. A great amount of resources and time has been put into learning how our mind responds and even heals as thoughts are spoken out loud, discussed, and then altered if necessary. If you experience severe depression or anxiety, it is essential that you see a professional, as these conditions can be life threatening. Many of your thinking patterns were established throughout your childhood, creating pathways in your brain. As an adult, you tend to respond to your life situations by reentering the brain pathway that was previously created by your childhood experiences. In other words, you were taught how to think by your peers, caregivers, church leaders, school authorities, and other influential adults. Remember the "marching orders" that you identified earlier in the healing process? Those marching orders are established pathways.

Psychotherapy can help you identify irrational or dysfunctional thinking patterns that no longer work for you. The word "dysfunctional" simply means that something no longer functions effectively. Consulting with a skilled and trained psychotherapist can change the way you think.

In actuality, your old thought pathways become inactive as you develop new pathways. You can lose what you no longer use. These newly created thought patterns will absolutely result in changes in your world because changing what you have comes from changing what you think. By the way, make sure that your therapist has a therapist and that your therapist has done his or her own healing work. A therapist cannot give something they do not have and they cannot take you down a road they have not traveled.

Support Groups

Learning to live in abundance always focuses on a glass that is half full, not a glass that is half empty.

Support groups can be additional learning tools on your journey into abundant living. Not only are you in the company of others who have had similar childhood and life experiences, but also support groups can be an effective way to learn adult thinking patterns that are nonshaming. It is important for a person to find a support group that is solution-based rather than a group that loves to commiserate about life problems. Learning to live in abundance always focuses on a glass that is half full, not a glass that is half empty.

Twelve-step support groups are particularly helpful in empowering individuals to change their lives by trusting in a loving Higher Power and living life differently. These groups teach individuals to cease viewing themselves as adult victims of others so that they can live a life that is happy, joyous, and free. The groups are based on the twelve steps of Alcoholics Anonymous and offer a design for living that includes working the steps, slogans, sponsorship, service to others, prayer, self-inventories, literature, and group meetings. There are different groups for various life issues including help for addictions, eating disorders, mental disorders, and family members who are affected by a range of disorders and mental illnesses. Without a doubt, twelve-step groups have helped many individuals and saved many lives.

The following is a list of well-known twelve-step groups:

- Alcoholics Anonymous is a group designed to help those struggling with alcohol dependency.

- Narcotics Anonymous is for people who struggle with a substance dependency and have difficulty relating to the specifics of alcohol addiction.

- There are other chemical dependency groups, such as Cocaine Anonymous, Crystal Meth Anonymous, and Marijuana Anonymous.

- Groups that address behavioral compulsions are Gamblers Anonymous, Eating Disorders Anonymous, Overeaters Anonymous, Sexual Compulsives Anonymous, Clutters Anonymous, Debtors Anonymous, and Workaholics Anonymous.

- Groups such as Al-Anon, Nar-Anon, Families Anonymous, Codependents Anonymous, and Adult Children of Alcoholics are for family members and friends whose lives have been affected by alcoholism, drug addiction, and other compulsive behaviors or mental disorders.

I strongly urge you to attend one of these support groups if your experiences include any of the above-mentioned issues. I have been attending a twelve-step group for the past fifteen years, and I plan on attending my group until I leave this world. These meetings substantiate my preciousness, help to maintain my connection to my all-loving Higher Power, and reinforce my adult thinking patterns. Try it. You may really like it.

Chapter Nine Exercises:
What You Can Do

S ince this whole section is about "doing the work," and this chapter specifically focuses on "unlocking the possibilities," take some time and sit with yourself to define the intentions that you want to incorporate into your life.

Here's an overview of what is detailed in this chapter:

Healthy Intentions for Your Life: Swallow one conceptual bite at a time:

Healthy Relationships—A healthy relationship is one based on desire instead of need. It is important to be happy with yourself, away from a significant other relationship, before you will be able to find an abundant relationship.

Exercise—Spend some quality time with *you*—make a weekly date with yourself and rediscover why it is that you are awesome to be with.

Financial Security—Understand that money is a medium of exchange rather than a badge of honor that represents your value to the world.

Physical Health—In order to live abundantly, you must be as healthy as you can be. It is important to practice healthy eating habits, exercise regularly, receive adequate sleep, and set aside time for relaxation and downtime.

Satisfying Career Pursuits—If you hate your job, find a new one. You absolutely cannot live in abundance unless you really like what you do as a career.

Emotional and Mental Health—Adult emotional maturity lies in the "cradle of moderation," balancing the selfish and selfless ends of the continuum.

Finding Your Center: It's an inside (and an outside) job:

Learn to thrive mentally and emotionally by nurturing yourself from the inside with meditation and breathing and from the outside with external resources such as therapy and support groups. There is no wrong recipe for emotional success—the only rule is that you have your own best interest in mind.

- **Meditation**
  Concentrative Meditation
  Mindfulness Meditation
- **Breathing Exercises**
- **Massage Therapy**
- **Individual or Group Psychotherapy**
- **Support Groups**

Ten

> *"No man can think clearly when*
> *his fists are clenched."*
>
> —George Jean Nathan—

*C*ameron first came to see me because John, her husband of seventeen years, told her that he wanted a divorce. John had been having an affair with a woman fifteen years younger than Cameron and he decided that he wanted to marry the other woman. Naturally Cameron was devastated and was extremely angry over her husband's infidelity. I spent many hours helping Cameron through the divorce and getting her to realize that she could create a new life and be happy. I was curious as to why Cameron was coming to see me a year later.

"Hi, Cameron," I said. "It is so nice to see you again. Tell me what has been going on in your world."

Cameron burst into tears as she tried to speak. "It is terrible," sobbed Cameron. "I thought that the divorce was bad, but this is even worse."

"What has happened?" I asked.

"I was just diagnosed with breast cancer," Cameron explained. "Here I am facing possible death and that sorry SOB is traveling around Europe with that young slut. You

*know, John actually married her three months after our divorce
was final. It is despicable and so trashy of both of them. How
could he?"*

*"I am so sorry, Cameron," I stated. "How bad is the
cancer?"*

*"Well, I have to do radiation and maybe chemotherapy,
but the doctors think there is a good chance that will take care
of it," Cameron reported. "I can hardly think about my body
healing because I am still so furious that John did this to me.
I hope his plane takes a nosedive into the Atlantic on the way
home from their trip. I can't even sleep at night even though I
am exhausted from all of my worry. When will he get what's
coming to him?"*

*I quickly realized that Cameron's biggest problem was
her fuming anger and resentment toward her ex-husband and
his new wife. "Cameron," I said. "We have got to get you to
a place of forgiveness toward John. The resentment that you
have toward him and his wife will literally eat your body and
will greatly impede its ability to heal."*

*"Forgive him?" Cameron yelled. "Are you crazy? I will
never forgive either one of them. I have made it my life's goal
to get back at them and make their lives as miserable as they
have made mine. If that is what you want me to do, then I
made a big mistake coming back to see you. I thought you were
on my side." Cameron put her head in her hands and started
crying uncontrollably.*

After a couple of minutes, Cameron's crying stopped.

*"Cameron," I said. "I know that you're sad, and I know
that you're angry about what happened between you and John.
It was not OK that he had an affair. Anyone would have the
same feelings that you are having. What I am worried about*

is that you are still stuck in some powerful resentments that are absolutely consuming you. I am on your side and that is the side of healing and living. Please do not allow the two of them to rob you of your healing and of your future. They are not worth it. I am asking you to trust me and let me guide you through this process so that you can finally be free from the affair."

Cameron nodded as more tears trickled down her cheeks. "OK," she said. "I will try."

"Good," I said. "That is all you have to do. You deserve to live."

Ten

Let Yourself Go:

Releasing Resentments and Connecting with a Higher Power

Each of us is meant to live a full and abundant life. Realizing your heart's desires can be as easy as believing that they already exist. As a child of God, everyone can access all of the prosperity the Universe has to offer. The Universe is unlimited and knows no boundaries. Realizing abundant success begins with mind action. Simply put, it can happen with the next right thought. Everyone, including you, has the ability to imagine and then realize his heart's desires.

This process sounds quite easy. Unfortunately many of us get stuck somewhere along the way. It isn't intentional, but life happens—and often not as we had planned or hoped. In order to experience abundance effectively, you must overcome a toxic shame core and you must let go of your resentments. Both are integral parts of the healing process. You have already begun to heal your shame core; now it is time to look at healing your resentments.

Resentment will block you from experiencing abundance because resentment is accompanied by never-ending anger, retaliation, and feelings of victimization. When you are stuck in these relentless feeling states, you send negative energy out into the universe and these feeling states and resulting behaviors will permeate all of your experiences. Your thinking may be so clouded by negativity that you fail to recognize opportunity and abundance even if it is right in front of you. You face the world with a scowl instead of a smile, and more than likely others will respond to you similarly. You reap what you sow.

You may be thinking, "Hey, wait a minute. As a child, I was the victim of abuse or insufficient nurturing. You have been telling me that my childhood experiences were not OK. You have been telling me to feel my feelings. Now you are telling me that I am not a victim? I don't get it." Let me explain.

You were victimized as a child and it is natural for you to have feelings of anger, fear, and pain. Resentment occurs when the original feelings of victimization are repeatedly reexperienced with growing intensity and you continue to feel victimized. This will block your ability to attract abundance. Remember what we said about feeling your feelings and then being able to step into acceptance. As you feel your feelings appropriately, they will dissipate and lose their intensity.

When I recall some episodes from my childhood or even some from adulthood, I know that what I experienced was not OK. If any anger arises, I breathe in and blow it out. I realize that my offenders were wounded themselves and did what they did out of their own woundedness. When I think about my offenders in this light, I feel compassion for them as wounded children. This thinking enables me to replace anger with compassion.

Remember, there are no bad people. There are wounded, shame-based children that grow up offending others as a way to pull themselves out of their shame.

Compassion is love, so I am releasing love into the universe as opposed to releasing fear, anger, or overwhelming sadness. As I express love, I will then receive love. If you are stuck in overwhelming anger, I recommend that you either get a photograph of your offender or imagine him or her as a child. Look into the eyes of the offender in the photograph or imagine the offender's child image standing in your presence. See his or her preciousness. Remember, there are no bad people. There are wounded, shame-based children that grow up offending others as a way to pull themselves out of their shame. This process does take time, so be easy on yourself. You will eventually get this concept and you will be able to incorporate this type of compassion into your adult experiences.

Forgiveness is something that you learn to do for yourself. It is a gift you bestow upon yourself so that you can live life abundantly. You do not get over your childhood abuse; rather, you get through the abuse by feeling the feelings and then letting them go. Staying stuck in those resentments will bind you to the person who originally caused the harm or the perceived harm. The perpetrator is not affected by the victim's obsessive thinking and is often busy living his or her own life. The victim, on the other hand, keeps reexperiencing anger and pain, which blocks his joy. Remember, abundance comes to us as we live life joyfully. The objective of forgiveness is not to let the perpetrator off the hook; rather, it is to get *you* off the hook. You will be able to get your life back. You are simply saying, "I love myself enough to stop reliving the occurrence and feeling the feelings that I felt when the original harmful or hurtful experience occurred. In setting you free, I set myself free."

You can help yourself clear resentments by taking a written resentment inventory. This process will allow you to clearly see past painful incidents and realize how you were threatened. This is a process that is used in twelve-step programs as an important part of recovery. By taking this inventory you can categorize past hurts and begin to heal them. Remember, you are engaging in this process so that you can live in abundance.

Write the following headings on a piece of paper: "Who Do I Resent," "What Happened," and "What Part of My Security Was Threatened (physical, emotional, spiritual, financial, or social)." Fill in the columns with the experiences that cause you to resent your offender. List all of the resentments that you can think of so that your inventory is thorough. This inventory format is adapted from the *Alcoholics Anonymous Big Book*. The following is an example of a partial resentment inventory:

Resentment Inventory Example		
Who Do I Resent?	What Happened?	What Part of My Security Was Threatened? (Physical, Emotional, Spiritual, Financial, Social)
My step-father	He ignored me.	Emotional, Financial
My spouse	He did not take me on a honeymoon.	Emotional, Financial, Social
My uncle	He sexually abused me as a child.	Emotional, Social, Spiritual, Physical
My minister	He taught me that God was to be feared.	Emotional, Spiritual
My childhood friends	They teased me about my freckles.	Emotional, Social

Once you have made a resentment inventory, you can then bless and release each of the offenders. Blessing your offenders is important because it releases them to their Higher Power. It could be something like "I bless you now and let you go." Every time the resentment recurs, go straight to the blessing so that you can release your offenders once again. Being chained to someone who has caused you pain gives them your internal power, the power to live life happy, joyous, and free. You may need to repeat the blessing many times as you are releasing and healing old resentments.

Connecting with a Higher Being

Along with releasing resentments, I also believe that developing a connection with a Higher Power is paramount to living abundantly. Considering the possibility that something larger than you exists (such as a loving Divine Intelligence who wants you to experience life to the fullest) is tremendously helpful in overcoming the belief that you do not deserve abundance.

For most people, the thought that you must do it all on your own is overwhelming. It is entirely too much pressure. You will feel a great sense of relief and security in knowing that there is a loving power that runs through the universe and is willing and able to provide you with guidance, opportunity, and endless acceptance. It matters not what name you give to your Higher Power. Call it God, the Universe, Energy, a Life Force, Nature, or whatever your intuition tells you is right for you. Some people find it easier to connect with a Higher Power that is a "she" rather than a "he." It is what it is, regardless of shape, size, name, or gender.

Serendipity is, in my opinion, your ability to tap into the opportunities that have been placed in your path by your Higher Power. They are not there by accident. They are there to help provide you with the ways and means of achieving your goals and receiving the desires of your heart.

You may find it easy to believe in the existence of Divine Intelligence. If so, then you were likely raised by parents who had relatively sound spiritual beliefs, or perhaps you attended a church that spoke of an unconditionally loving God who does not judge. If you are one of those people, cheers! The process of understanding that you deserve and will be led to experience abundance is much easier for you. If this is not the case for you, the process may be slightly more difficult. But take heart—with a little time and effort, you *will* be able to grow into your own spiritual knowing.

If you were raised in a religious system that was shame based, you may need to reconstruct a new concept of God. This was my experience. Although the word "God" felt right for me, I knew that I needed to completely let go of a judgmental God and create a loving God. I accomplished this in a couple of ways. First, I decided that I needed to start from scratch. I determined that the shame-based messages I had heard were totally false and were fear based. Because I had been an avid Bible student, I went through the Bible and wrote down on index cards only the scriptures that had to do with God's love. I carried those cards in my purse so that I could read them whenever the opportunity arose. There is no telling how many times I read those cards. I literally had to brainwash myself into a different conviction that consisted solely of a loving God.

Secondly, I decided to read books about other religions and different concepts of spirituality. I read about Buddhism and other Eastern philosophies. I read the Bhagavad Gita, the Koran, and books by Wayne W. Dyer, Marianne Williamson, Deepak Chopra, and Thomas Merton, to name only a few. What I came to believe was that everyone was basically saying the same thing; they just worded it differently.

I also became an observer of nature, recognizing that the beauty of nature and the miracles apparent in the very existence of that beauty represented God's love. I came to believe that God was God and that this Power loved me and thought that I rocked! It was that simple. I loved my new awareness as it settled into my soul. I continue to keep it really simple because my mind can get carried away with trying to figure it all out. When my mind tries to be too "smart," I can start to doubt, and I don't want that to happen. I shifted from a *belief* into a *knowing* that I felt permeating every cell in my body. I still have that feeling. It literally runs through my veins and is my life force. Searching for your *own* truth will be worth the effort, so start searching.

Once you come to settle into a belief that feels comfortable, you have begun to experience a spiritual awakening. You are learning to understand that you are a spiritual being having a human experience. You are learning to believe that you are an extension of your Higher Power and you can recognize that others are an extension of their Higher Power.

We are all connected because we are all "of" the same source. We are literally brothers and sisters with every other human being. As you connect with an all-loving Divine Being, you will begin to have faith in the goodness of life, no matter how it all appears. Faith will give you hope— hope for today and hope for tomorrow. I love the following definition of faith:

"To trust in the force that moves the universe is faith.
Faith isn't blind; it's visionary. Faith is believing that the
universe is on our side and that the universe knows what it's doing.
Faith is a psychological awareness of an unfolding force for
good, constantly at work in all dimensions."
—Author unknown—

Your spiritual journey will last a lifetime as it continues to change and grow. I suggest that you start and end your day with spiritual readings so that you stay tuned into your spiritual awareness. Once you taste it, you cannot be separated from it. Even if you occasionally do not feel it, it is there. Stay in your practice of spirituality and you will feel it again.

Chapter Ten Exercises:
What You Can Do

Releasing resentments and connecting with a Higher Power is not as easy as it sounds. The feelings of angst we carry with us toward people who wronged us in childhood are rigid. It's like when you have scar tissue after a physical trauma—it needs to be worked out with repetitive physical therapy exercises. You will never gain full range of motion without pushing yourself and getting a little uncomfortable. The same is true for our built-up emotional scars. We simply have to work through them in order to move on. Remember, the objective of forgiveness is not to let the perpetrator off the hook; rather, it is to get you off the hook.

Exercise (detailed earlier in this chapter): Take your written resentment inventory to help you clear resentments and begin to wrap your brain around the abundance that awaits you.

V

Living in Abundance:
You Absolutely Deserve It

Eleven

"The lure of the distant and the difficult is deceptive. The great opportunity is where you are."
—John Burroughs—

I walked into my therapist's office and sat down on his blue leather couch. My divorce was under way, and I was beginning to think that I would survive the ending of my marriage. The anger, sadness, and fear were no longer consuming me, and I was actually having moments of feeling joy.

"Well, Janice, so what are you planning to do now?" my therapist asked.

"What do you mean?" I questioned.

"I mean, what do you want to do with the rest of your life? Your children will all be out of the house in five years and you will still have a lot of time to do whatever you want," he explained. "Have you ever thought about going back to school and possibly becoming a therapist? I think you would be really good at it."

"I guess I haven't given any thought to how I really want my life to look from this point forward," I said. "I do have the desire to use my painful experience as a way to help others *and I have always loved school. Do you think I am too old to start a career?"*

"Absolutely not," he responded. "You can't sit around and do nothing. You'd be bored to tears. You should check it out and see what you think."

From that point forward, I was off and running. I started attending graduate school and although it was somewhat difficult to remember how to study for an exam, I loved every minute of it. During my time in school, I worked at a judicial treatment center with men who had been convicted of drug-related felonies and had drug addiction problems of their own. After completing the coursework, I worked at a mental hospital pro bono and stayed there for a year because it gave me incredible experience. Later I worked at a court-ordered outpatient treatment center for about six months.

All of these opportunities became available to me in rather miraculous, effortless ways and with absolute perfect timing. During this process, I kept thinking that I wanted to start a private practice, but most importantly, I just wanted to make a difference in the lives of others. I repeatedly said to the Universe, "I will go wherever You want me to go, and I will do whatever You want me to do. Just show me."

Four years after starting graduate school, I had my license. One afternoon, I called my former therapist.

"I need your advice on an opportunity to rent some office space from an acquaintance of mine. This appears to be a pretty good deal for me, but I am not sure about the location," I explained. "The space is in an office park that I am not crazy about and it is farther away from my house than I would like. I really want to be somewhere with more activity."

"Yes, I agree that the location is not particularly desirable," he said. "Maybe one of the therapists in my office would be willing to let you pay to use their office on Saturdays or on a day when they are not working. I will run it by them." His office was five minutes from my house and was above a beautiful and thriving strip center with restaurants, shops, and plenty of parking. The therapists agreed to let me use their office and my private practice was set in motion.

I began by calling one of the psychiatrists with whom I had worked at the mental hospital and told him that I was in business on my own. A week later, he referred one of his patients to me and I started seeing the referral on Saturday mornings. My practice steadily grew, and a year later we expanded the space so that I could have an office of my own. The rest is history.

With a desire in my heart, I took action to accomplish the task before me. I visualized what I wanted and God took care of the details. I never doubted what I wanted or God's ability and willingness to guide me. I focused on doing what was in front of me and I lived one day at a time. I adore my job and I know that I am doing exactly what I was created to do. How sweet it is!

Eleven

Thinking Big:

Go Forth and Prosper

---

*When I tell you to be full of yourself, I want you
to be full of your self-value, which is not selfish at all.*

You deserve to experience abundance. Have you read that before? I have written that many times because I want you to experience what I have experienced. Sometimes it is really difficult for people to truly believe that they deserve abundance. You may have been taught that it was selfish to want it all. Your family system might have told you that to be selfless was honorable. When I tell you to be full of yourself, I want you to be full of your *self-value*, which is not selfish at all. Everyone deserves abundance and everyone deserves to experience true joy and happiness while living a full and richly rewarding life.

You do not want abundance at the expense of others. Now that would be selfish. The truth is that each individual must seek abundance on his or her own. You cannot seek it for the world, and the world cannot seek it for you.

Once your thoughts are aligned toward getting what you desire, nothing can hold you back. In order to successfully embrace this concept, you must first clear your mind of any negative thoughts or feelings about living abundantly. The following truths will help you understand abundant thinking as you move in the direction of abundant living.

Prosperity is your birthright.

You are worthy of all you wish to experience simply because you were born. As a child of your personal Higher Power, you are entitled to unlimited prosperity and abundance. Considering your noble birthright, I want you to imagine that no desire is too big or too small for the Universe to fulfill. If God is a king, then you are a prince or a princess. From birth, each of us is meant to live as abundantly as we desire. To fully embrace this concept, you must begin to see yourself in a deserving light. By applying the concepts in this book, you have begun to understand and release old thinking, feeling, and behavioral patterns. You now understand the shame core and you have started the healing process. You have wrapped your arms around your precious wounded child and you are seeing yourself in a much more positive light. Remember, you can claim prosperity simply because you exist.

Release guilt about being prosperous.

Understanding and believing that prosperity is your birthright is the first step to actually experiencing abundance. After settling into this belief, you may feel guilty about thinking abundantly. As you look at the world and all of the people who have so little, you may ask yourself, "Why should I have prosperity, joy, and love in my life when so many others experience lack in these areas?" Again, you are replaying old tapes that taught you to compare your life with the lives of others.

When you compare, you will always lose. Your upbringing or life experiences have shaped how you see your life today, and the resulting feelings are guilt and shame. If you feel guilty or unworthy of what you desire, the guilt will block your success. Guilt is a powerful emotion that has the ability to keep you stuck.

Thoughts are compelling mind actions that will determine the outcome of what you imagine. If you think you are not worthy or deserving of something, then chances are you will achieve lackluster results that match your thoughts. As you begin to take responsibility for your guilty thoughts and throw them away, you will notice that asking for what you desire becomes easier. With some practice, it is just as easy to focus your attention on what you want as it is to focus on what you don't want. Remember, if your needs are not immediately met, have faith. The good that you desire is coming to you.

Understand and release beliefs that no longer suit your new prosperous way of thinking.
More often than not, people do certain things out of habit. Our thoughts are no exception. What you believe and how you respond is often second nature. Responses can be part of an old belief system, perhaps from childhood experiences or habits you picked up in your daily living. As you begin to see yourself in the new light of prosperity, you will recognize beliefs that don't fit your life anymore. By releasing resentments and guilty thoughts, you can begin to let go of old, dysfunctional belief systems. Doing so will pave the way toward abundant living.

Your perception about money probably developed from your family system. Perhaps you were raised in poverty and had parents who constantly talked about lack and limitation, as if there was never enough to meet the family needs. Or maybe you had parents who tried to get everything for a bargain. Trying to get everything for a bargain creates an impregnable poverty complex. Perhaps your parents even talked about rich people as being greedy or evil. They may have had a sense of "poverty pride." As you now know, this is completely untrue. Greed or evil thoughts and actions can exist regardless of someone's monetary status. Greed is about hoarding what you have and having resentments toward those who have more.

Abundance is not confined solely to financial prosperity. You probably desire abundant love, health, joy, and friendship as well as financial security. Your "stinking thinking" about limitation is what keeps you poor in many areas of your life. Once you see yourself as prosperous, abundance will flow to you and meet your desires.

Abundant Thinking Versus Shame-Based Thinking

As you can see, your very own thoughts can sabotage the life you desire. With some work, you can begin to reframe your focus on getting what you want and desire. Some examples of how easily we can turn a negative outlook into a positive one are as follows:

Letting Things Happen Versus Making Things Happen

Trying to make things happen is an illusion of control, which can often result in frustration—kind of like you are trying to put a square peg into a round hole. By working too hard to make things happen, the result is often painful and less than what you truly wanted and deserve. Conversely, letting things gently unfold comes from self-esteem and trusting in a loving Higher Power. An easier and more effective approach is to breathe, relax, and let things unfold exactly as planned for you. You do the footwork and then leave the results up to Divine Intelligence.

Attitude of Gratitude Versus Attitude of Lack

Whatever you focus on will grow, so when you ruminate about the negative aspects of your life, you will continue to experience negative circumstances. You will slip into feeling sorry for yourself as you approach life from a half-empty perspective as opposed to a half-full perspective. Feeling sorry for yourself results in self-pity, and having a "pity party" for yourself is quite lonely. No one else really wants to be in attendance. Self-pity is a choice, and the way out of self-pity is gratitude—thinking about what you *do* have.

Self-pity and gratitude cannot occupy the same space in your thinking.

Gratitude is not only the cure for self-pity but is essential if you want to have more of something. An effective way to develop your ability to live in gratitude is to write a gratitude list. Start by thinking of something for which you are grateful that corresponds with every letter of the alphabet. Your gratitude list might look something like the following:

A – I am thankful for apples and my sister Ann.

B – I am thankful for my healthy body.

C – I am thankful for my children and my church.

You can mentally create a gratitude list when you are doing another activity such as when you are driving or taking a walk, but try to actually write your list whenever possible. The written word is extremely powerful. As you write your gratitude list, you will begin to focus on the positive things in your life. By the time you get to the letter "L" you will probably find yourself in a better frame of mind. Self-pity and gratitude cannot occupy the same space in your thinking.

Your attitude, which is your thinking, will greatly affect what happens in your life. You have the power to change your attitude. People are drawn to those who have a positive attitude. Those people exude an uplifting energy that is contagious. You want more of them. You can fake it until you make it by waking up every morning and saying, "Good morning, God," as opposed to saying, "Good God, it's morning."

"The longer I live, the more I realize the impact of attitude on life. Attitude, to me, is more important than facts. It is more important than the past, than education, than money, than circumstances, than failures, than successes, than what other people think or say or do. It is more important than appearance, giftedness, or skill. It will make or break a company, a church, a home. The remarkable thing is we have a choice every day regarding the attitude we will embrace for that day. We cannot change our past; we cannot change the fact that people will act in a certain way. We cannot change the inevitable. The only thing we can do is play on the one string we have, and that is our attitude. I am convinced that life is ten percent what happens to me and ninety percent how I react to it. And so it is with you . . . we are in charge of our attitudes."
—Charles Swindoll—

Peaceful Thinking Versus a Racing Brain

If you struggle with a racing brain, it is probably the result of trying to figure it all out. Attempting to figure everything out is a monumental task that is impossible to accomplish as well as being absolutely exhausting.

When you find yourself in an in-between place such as between jobs or between relationships, your brain may go into overload because of the unknown as it relates to the future. Actually, we never really know anything other than what happened in the past and what is happening now. Because of the unknown, you may find yourself feeling anger, fear, or pain. A racing brain is typically the result of one of these feelings. Rather than feeling the fear, pain, or anger and then making a decision based on intuition blended with the facts of a situation, you may find yourself remaining stuck in your racing thoughts. The more your brain races, the more your brain races.

Being at peace and letting things unfold will produce far less stress. To do nothing is to do something, and it is often the most powerful thing you can do. Some steps to calm your racing brain are deep breathing, meditation, identifying what you are feeling, blowing the feeling out of your open mouth, and then saying a calming prayer or mantra. With practice, these actions will slow down your brain and corral your obsessive thoughts. Don't let a mind trip trip you out!

Could Versus Should

"Could" will open the door to all possibilities and personal choice. "Should," on the other hand, results in shame and represents living from duty and the choices of others. Choice is important in all areas of your life, especially in your relationships and job. Giving yourself permission to make a choice keeps you from feeling stuck and like a victim. If you have the choice to leave, then you can choose to stay. If you choose to stay, you must give up your right to blame other people or circumstances for your restlessness or unhappiness.

There are no mistakes, only learning experiences.

Notice how your body feels when you say "could." There is an internal and uplifting energy that accompanies the word "could." You now have a choice as to what will work best for you and whether or not you really want to do something. Now notice how your body feels when you say "should." There is a heaviness that accompanies the word "should." This heaviness is a warning sign telling you that you have stepped into shame. The same is true when using "could" and "should" in the past tense. If you say to yourself, "I could have done . . ." you open yourself up to examining something you have already chosen and then giving yourself a choice as to whether or not you would do the same thing again. Rather than beating yourself up over a past decision, you are giving yourself the opportunity to learn the lesson and then throw away the experience. If you say to yourself, "I should have done . . ." you will feel less than, stupid, or inadequate, all of which represent shame. You can easily get stuck in deep regret by viewing past experiences as mistakes. There are no mistakes, only learning experiences. Don't "should" on yourself or on other people! It can be really messy.

How Interesting Versus How Horrible

When circumstances happen that are beyond your control and you perceive them as being bad or even horrible, you have stepped out of living in abundance and are back into living in lack. You have clothed yourself in what I call the "life sucks coat," a coat that is heavy, stinky, and extremely unattractive. Fortunately you can take off the coat and reframe your thinking at any given time.

If there is an all-loving Divine Intelligence, then everything that happens has got to be good, even if it is impossible to see the good at the time of the event. By changing your perspective from "how horrible" to "how interesting," you make yourself open to the good that *will* happen as a result of any particular occurrence. This does not mean that you won't have certain inevitable feelings that are very real. You are human. What I am saying is that after you recover from the shock of the situation and feel the fear, anger, and sadness, you can say to yourself, "I may not like the way things have happened, but it will be interesting to see what good can come from all of this." You may make some life changes that you have been postponing, repair some relationships that were in need of repair, or find an opportunity presenting itself to you that would have been impossible without the perceived tragedy. The possibilities are endless.

During the downward spiral of my marriage and resulting divorce, I was devastated. Looking back, however, I realize that all of those experiences were preparing me to be the counselor that I am today. They were my "graduate school of life" experiences that graced me with the ability to relate to my clients as they entered my office in their own fear, sadness, and pain. It took me some time to realize the goodness and reap the accompanying benefits, but they came nonetheless. Without my gloomy past, there could not be my glorious present.

Keeping an Open Mind Versus Black-and-White Thinking

Many of us were raised in a family system that taught us to think in extremes: right or wrong, good or bad, all or nothing, my way or the highway. We were not trained to see the world from a more moderate point of view. Learning to keep an open mind about the differences in other people as well as external circumstances will keep you in a much more serene place and open you to the unlimited possibilities that are before you. You will be better able to adjust to changes as they occur.

I often hear people talk about resisting change in their life, when in actuality nothing really ever stays the same. Change is continually occurring whether you like it or not. You are not the same today as you were yesterday or, for that matter, five minutes ago. The Buddha said that change is inevitable but suffering is optional. It is our resistance to change (rather than change itself) that creates suffering. Keeping an open mind and having an attitude of acceptance will allow your Higher Power to bring to you the abundance that you desire and deserve.

Separateness Versus Enmeshment

Separateness is the practice of boundaries. Implementing a healthy boundary system will keep you from becoming enmeshed with other people. The saying "If mama ain't happy, ain't nobody happy" is the essence of enmeshment. Everyone around the unhappy mama is taking on mama's stuff: her sadness, fear, guilt, or shame. As you implement a boundary system, you will be able to realize that another person's experiences, thoughts, feelings, behaviors, values, etc., are not your own. This doesn't mean that you do not have compassion for the person in their unhappiness. The word compassion means "with love." You can have compassion for them and love them without losing yourself to their experience. You can watch what they are feeling, for example, without sucking in their feelings as your own.

When my youngest daughter went away to college, she called me one morning in tears. She told me she was really homesick. I talked with her for a little while, and then we hung up the phone to go about our day. I was very sad for the entire day, wishing that I could do something to "fix" her sadness. In the early evening, I called her back to see how she was feeling. She answered the telephone sounding happy and excited. When I asked her how her day had been, she answered, "Great!" She said that she and one of her friends had seen something really funny shortly after we had spoken that had changed her mood from sadness to joy. I had literally sucked in her sadness all the way from Kansas to Dallas! Rather than having compassion for her and leaving it at that, I had felt her sadness all day long. I had lost myself, my joy, in what I perceived as being her emotional reality.

When other people are experiencing negativity, imagine yourself in a jelly jar. Watch them in their experiences without taking in their negativity. Ask yourself, "Is this what I am feeling? Is this what I am thinking?" If it is not yours, then do not let it in. Allow their experiences and feelings to bounce off your jelly jar and then float away. It is not that you don't care. Of course you care when people are experiencing something that causes them to feel sadness, fear, or pain, but realize that it is not your experience. It is not yours to "fix."

Perceiving that you need to fix someone is emotional caretaking and that is simply no longer your duty. You are really needing and wanting them to feel differently so that you can feel differently. It is no one's job to make you feel anything. That is you needing to control them. When you stop trying to make everyone happy, you are allowing others the dignity of their own experiences. You stop playing God. Their reality is not about you, although it may affect you and your experience. It is really none of your business. It is not on your side of the street. You can have compassion for them without sucking in their stuff.

A boundary system also includes containing your own stuff so that others do not take it in and try to fix you. As you practice keeping yourself from trying to change others, you will realize that it is not other people's duty to take on your experiences and make you better. You can tell others that it is not their job to take care of you, thus releasing them from trying to accomplish an impossible task. In her book *Facing Codependence*, Pia Mellody does a wonderful job of explaining the details of boundaries. She taught me all that I know about boundaries, and for that I am eternally grateful.

Intuitiveness Versus Intellectualizing

Our intuition was created at birth. Rather than being taught to honor your intuition and develop the capacity to tap into your intuition, you were probably taught to ignore or at least minimize it. Our world loves a great thinker. We learn to think about a problem or opportunity endlessly, examining all aspects and possibilities, but what we often miss is what our intuition is leading us to do.

Your intuition resides deep in your gut and is your guidance system. As you leave your childhood wounds and begin to live from a place of self-esteem, you can begin to trust your intuition as you make decisions. You learn to combine your gut feelings with your ability to think rationally as opposed to intellectualizing decisions based purely on your thoughts and disregarding any feeling component.

When trying to make a choice, stop and ask yourself, "What does my gut tell me to do?" Ask yourself what you would feel if you implemented your choice. Would you feel fear, guilt, sadness, joy, love, anger? When making a change, it is normal to feel a small amount of anxiety or fear. But if the feeling is significant, that is your intuition telling you that this is not the best decision, at least for the time being. After you have determined your feeling or combination of feelings, look at the facts of the situation combined with the feelings and see if you have clarity about the choice. If you do not know what to do, then do nothing until your feelings change or the facts of the situation change. Your intuition may not tell you what to do, but it will always tell you what not to do. Honor it.

Spiritual Advocate Versus Spiritual Adversary

Those who were raised with religious abuse and shame may view God as an adversary. Abundance is realizing that God, the Universe, or a Higher Power is our advocate and longs to partner with us as we live our life in rich abundance. Realizing this truth instills hope. With omnipotence, love, and wisdom as my partners, I can begin to entertain unlimited possibilities. As your concept of a Higher Power solidifies, it will become easier to view your Higher Power as an advocate. Hopefully the thoughts and activities discussed in chapter ten have helped you to view God as your partner in finances, health, love, and life skills in general. Remember, your God is a God of abundance, not a God of reduction.

Blessing Others Versus Criticizing Others

When you criticize others, you enter a negative frame of mind and no longer come from a place of self-esteem. You try to make yourself feel better than them as a way to pull yourself out of shame. Criticism of others will block your ability to attract abundance because you are releasing negative energy into the universe. Negative energy has the ability to wall you off from the good that is coming to you.

Something that I have noticed about myself is that whenever I am being critical of someone else, it is a warning signal that I am being critical of myself. Self-criticism leads to criticism of others. When a critical thought about another person enters my mind, I try to stop that thought and replace it by asking myself how I have been criticizing myself. Maybe I looked in the mirror earlier in the day and told myself that I do not look very good and then later in the day I find myself mentally criticizing what another person is wearing. I will then tell myself that I am precious and beautiful. As my thoughts shift from self-criticism to self-love, it is much easier to look at others through the eyes of love. I am learning to be full of myself—self-love, self-acceptance, self-esteem. An exercise that will help to develop your ability to cease criticism is to practice the following mantra:

Today I will criticize no one, including myself.

Fear and Worry Versus Trust

Fear and worry block our ability to live in the now where we can make decisions that foster abundance. A wonderful acronym for fear that encapsulates its meaning is:

False
Experiences
Appearing
Real

Action will always help abolish fear.

When a person is worrying, he is living in fear. He is literally making things up in his mind that are negative and then expecting them to happen. He is "awful-izing" his future and anticipating the resulting pain. A technique that will help you eliminate worry is to list what you fear. After the fears are on paper, look at each fear and determine whether or not any action can be taken today that will help eliminate the possibility of the event actually occurring. List the steps, if any, that need to be taken and then develop a timetable for taking the action. Action will always help abolish fear. If there is no action to be taken, put the list of fears into a God box, and trust that your Higher Power will take care of you and guide you in the future to take needed action.

Another antidote for fear is prayer. Prayer is your way to communicate with your Higher Power and relieve you of your fearful thinking. One of my favorite prayers is The Serenity Prayer:

God, grant me the serenity
To accept the things I cannot change,
The courage to change the things I can,
And the wisdom to know the difference.

Learning to let go of the future and the past is how you learn to live in today, which is where you will experience abundance. Spending time worrying about what *might* happen or regretting past decisions and experiences is time wasted. Abundant life and abundant opportunities will present themselves to you in the precious present. It is the only time you have. I strongly suggest that you memorize or at least add the following to your daily meditation period. Say or read it daily as a way to help you learn to "let go and let God" and practice living one day at a time.

"Spiritual consciousness is continually
'replenishing' its earth. We must never try to hold on,
mentally, to present conditions or particular objects.
As long as such things belong to us by right of consciousness
they will stay, and nothing can separate them from us.

If they go, it is really because we have outgrown them, and something better is coming.
Let them go freely and without regret, for until they are gone the better thing cannot make its appearance."
—Author unknown—

Chapter Eleven Exercises:
What You Can Do

You deserve abundance. It's time to take what is yours. Review this chapter as often as you need to reiterate how deserving you are.

Remind yourself of the truths that will help you understand abundant thinking as you move in the direction of abundant living:

- Prosperity is your birthright.
- Release guilt about being prosperous.
- Understand and release beliefs that no longer suit your new prosperous way of thinking.

You will stumble along the way, as we all do. Keep this information in your emotional toolbox as you recognize and practice abundant thinking rather than shame-based thinking:

- Letting things happen versus making things happen
- Attitude of gratitude versus attitude of lack *

*Exercise (detailed earlier in this chapter): Write and rewrite your gratitude list

- Peaceful thinking versus a racing brain
- Could versus should
- How interesting versus how horrible
- Keeping an open mind versus black-and-white thinking
- Separateness versus enmeshment
- Intuitiveness versus intellectualizing

- Spiritual advocate versus spiritual adversary
- Blessing others versus criticizing others
- Fear and worry versus trust

Twelve

"I want to get you excited about who you are, what you are, what you have, and what can still be for you. I want to inspire you to see that you can go far beyond where you are right now."

—Virginia Satir—

I grew up in a very chaotic household. My father was an alcoholic who was never "available emotionally" and was obsessed with saving money. He always said we were poor even though he made millions of dollars. This was very confusing to me as a child. My mother was an emotional mess who was obsessed with trying to stop my father from drinking. Pretty much, we did not have parents or caregivers. Luckily I had two sisters, one older and one younger, who were there to support me. We were all very close and are still close to this day. My parents ended up getting a divorce when I was fifteen years old, but most of the shame and abuse had already occurred. I was a wounded child.

As a child, I was always very scared and could never sleep alone at night. I thought that someone was going to kidnap me or murder me. Since my parents were not there to comfort me, I had to survive on my own. The only thing that made my anxiety go away and made me feel safe was to make all of my "stuff" perfect. I developed obsessive-compulsive disorder

(OCD), which was a coping mechanism for my anxiety and fear. Being the middle child, I also became a caretaker for my sisters and my mother. Instead of my mother mothering me, I mothered her.

Before I healed my inner wounded child and the shame that lived deep in my soul, I always thought that I had to be perfect. My perfectionism continued into adulthood, and I also believed that I needed to save all of my money. I didn't feel valuable or worthy unless these things happened. I tried to control everything, even my husband. When my life felt out of control, my OCD and perfectionism would be in full effect. I never realized that this behavior was not coming from the "adult" me but from the wounded child within me. It saved my life to heal the inner child and to comfort her. Now she knows that the adult me is here to always take care of her. She has nothing to fear.

After working to heal the shame, I began to use affirmations to help shape me into a healthy adult. They truly became the source for restructuring my thinking. I put the affirmations in a place where I could see them and read them daily so they could become a part of me and my everyday life. Whenever I would start to doubt myself or feel shame creeping back into my soul, I'd say the affirmations over and over so they could become embedded in my brain. Previously I had read sayings once or twice and thought they would become part of my everyday living. However, once I healed the shame, everything changed and made sense. I realized my self-value and could therefore truly understand and believe the affirmations.

The affirmations are my saving grace and the template of how I want to live my new, healthy life. I am now operating as an adult and not like a child. I realize that the affirmations can become a part of my life, not just something I read. I understand that I had to totally believe that my Higher Power was my partner and would always be with me. I am not perfect, and I know there will be hard days. That is part of the human experience. But now I know I am never alone. At all times, I have my "child self" dancing on my shoulder with God next to me, leading us through life.

—Kristie

Twelve

Realizing Your Heart's Desire:

Make Your Own Waves

Enough time has been spent on the heavy lifting. You have examined your baggage, taken what you want to keep, and left the rest. It is time to put your baggage in storage and move on to the lighter part of life that is waiting for you with open arms.

You want to be happy, right?

You want to be happy, right? If the answer is yes, then it is important for you to decide what it is that will bring you happiness. These are the things that you want to attract into your life. The Universe has no limitations, so do not hold yourself back. The Universe is also plentiful, so do not concern yourself with whether or not there is enough to go around for everyone. It is never wrong to want something more or something different from what you currently have, so dream big.

The mind is a powerful tool, so picturing what you want has an amazing power to create. Remember that Divine Intelligence has your best interests at heart. If you don't get exactly what you want, you will get something better. "Not my will but Thy will" is a strong way to let go and allow your Higher Power to do its job.

The importance of taking action cannot be overstated. The actions you take in the general direction of what you desire will create the emotional energy that will help to jump-start the abundance process. There are several steps that will help you get the process started. As you implement the following suggestions, you will begin to see yourself in a new way, a way of abundance, prosperity, and fullness.

Step 1: Write Down Desires, Wants, and Goals

The first step in attracting what you desire is to write down what you want to experience and have in your life. The written word is very powerful and provides a road map to follow. Be specific in your desires because specificity will create excitement as you visualize your future. It will put a zip in your step as you anticipate the good.

Write about the areas in your life where you would like to experience improvements; these could include finances, career, health, relationships, personal or spiritual growth, or material desires. Use descriptive words and be as thorough as you can. You may want something as simple as a new dress. Write down what color you imagine the dress to be, the fabric it is made of, its particular style, and any special detailing it might have.

You may desire something bigger like your perfect mate, a new career, or a new house for your family. Make a list of the characteristics you desire and find appealing. If you desire a new house for your family you might write, "The house is a red brick colonial with white columns on a huge front porch. There are at least four bedrooms and three bathrooms, with plenty of room to entertain friends and loved ones. It has a large yard where my children can play, and it's furnished to my taste and satisfaction. The neighborhood is safe and quiet. The money to pay for it comes easily."

You can go to the river of abundance with either a thimble or a barrel. The choice is yours.

Although all things are possible, some things are more probable than others. I love to sing and dance, and I would love to perform in a Broadway musical. At age fifty-eight, however, it is not very probable. What I could do is be open to local theater if that were truly one of my heart's desires. Divine Intelligence can make a way where we can see no way, so dream big and be open to the unknown. Don't get tied up in the details of how it will come to pass. It is not up to the human spirit to assume the order of how things happen. Having faith that your request will be met in the right time and the right way is crucial. You can go to the river of abundance with either a thimble or a barrel. The choice is yours. Get excited about going to the river with a barrel and know that your heart's desires are coming to you now in the best way possible.

Step 2: Make a "Vision Board"

A vision board is a success map of your heart's desires. It is a visual representation of your specific goals, wants, and desires. It takes the mental pictures of what you desire and makes them visible. After you have written your desires, find photos or pictures that portray them. Use pictures that are colorful and descriptive. The Universe thrives on color. Just look around you—there is color everywhere. If you want a big, colorful life, use pictures that depict that life.

Create a board that can be divided into the areas of your life in which you desire change such as finances/career, love/relationships, personal/spiritual growth, health, etc. For example, if you long for financial growth, add play money or checks to the board. No amount is too big. Perhaps you desire a dream home. Find photos that look similar to your dream home. If you cannot find an accurate representation, add pictures that might show specific details or elements of your new home. If you desire a new mate, look for a picture of a person you find attractive who might meet your specific criteria. Although you may not find the exact house or marry the person in your picture, the Universe uses the pictures as a reference point so that it can go to work on meeting your specific requirements. Again, vibrant color pictures will more quickly set your dreams into action.

When making a vision board, be creative and leave plenty of space for additional desires. Make more than one vision board if needed. It is perfectly acceptable to create multiple success maps. Perhaps you have one for your family, one for your career, and one for material desires. After you have completed your vision board, place it somewhere you can reflect on it frequently, such as your bathroom mirror or a special place where you feel spiritually connected. Ponder your rich and rewarding life as it unfolds before your eyes.

As the Universe begins to fulfill your wishes, mark them off your wish list or write "Done" on that vision board item. Remember to thank your Higher Power for bringing you your heart's desires. Gratitude for what you have will bring you more of what you want. You will be amazed to see how quickly you start to see changes as life unfolds to bring you your longings.

Step 3: Visualize It: See It to Be It
Now that you have mapped out your desired path on your vision board, it is important to set aside five to ten minutes each day to focus clearly on your new destiny. By visualizing what you wish to receive, you will further solidify your coming abundance. It is best to visualize in a quiet, private space. I visualize in the morning (after I have had my cup of coffee, of course), but if you are usually rushed in the morning, later in the day may be better for you. I also set a timer so that I am not tempted to look at the clock. Sit in a comfortable chair and shut your eyes. Think about living the abundant life that you have laid out in words and pictures. Make sure that you see yourself in the picture. What are you wearing? How is your hair styled? Feel the

feelings that you will experience once you are living your dream. Do you have a gigantic smile on your face? Are tears of joy streaming down your face? The feelings are very important because they will turbo-charge change.

Visualize your desires accurately and vividly. For example, if you want a beautiful new car, picture yourself walking up to it. Open the door and get inside. What does the car smell like? Take in the features. Picture yourself driving to a particular destination. Maybe you are driving through the mountains or to the beach. What are you feeling? How does the car respond to your input? Are you listening to your favorite rock band or are you driving in silence? Is your family in the car or are you driving alone? Visualize any thoughts or feelings that will better connect you to your beautiful new car.

While visualizing your new life, you might think of something new or different that you want. Write it down and add it to your vision board so the Universe can get to work on that also.

Step 4: Prepare to Receive Your Heart's Desires by Taking Action

Preparing to receive what you want to have in your world actually signals to yourself and the Universe that you believe your desires are coming to you. You are taking action in the general direction of your dreams. It is like preparing for an invited guest to arrive. For example, if you want a new car, clean out your garage. You would not park the car of your dreams in a dirty garage that is cluttered and messy. Visit car dealerships that sell the car you desire. Walk around the car lot and pick out the color you want. Sit in the car that you would choose if you were buying the car. Smell the leather and feel the softness against your body. Take the car for a test drive and notice how you feel as you drive the car. Notice how the car handles the road. Be aware of how the steering wheel feels as you make a turn.

If you want to move into a different house, put your house on the market or drive around the neighborhood where you want to live. Notice the style of houses that you like. Can you see yourself living there? Clean out the drawers and cabinets in your current home, getting rid of the items that you would not take with you when you move.

If you want a new wardrobe, clean out your closet and donate the clothes that no longer suit you. You are helping others as well as making room for your new wardrobe. Walk around the store where you would buy your new wardrobe and notice the clothes that you would purchase. Feel the fabrics and even try on a few items so that you have a mental picture of yourself in the clothing.

If you desire a loving relationship, join a dating service or another group or activity where you will be around other single people with similar interests. Make a list of the characteristics that you want in your future partner. Notice the qualities in others that are important to you and work on having these same qualities yourself. Like attracts like. Visualize sitting on the couch or cooking dinner together in the kitchen. Think about how it will feel as you laugh and then embrace one another. Think about where you would travel together and collect pamphlets and pictures of that special place.

You would not order a hamburger and simply tell the cook to make it however he likes. You might not like it. Likewise, you would not order a partner (or any of your heart's desires) and leave the details up to fate.

If you take an action and it doesn't work, do not consider the action a failure. Think of the action as a stepping-stone toward abundance. What you experience today is not your tomorrow. Do not concern yourself with specific outcomes. Trust in the ultimate goodness of the Universe and believe that you deserve it. What you believe, you will receive!

Step 5: Abolish Doubt

As we've already discussed, negativity will block you from receiving what you want in your life. It is very important to eliminate as much negativity from your life as possible. Because the newspaper and news reports tend to dwell on negative things that are happening in our world, I strongly urge you to stop reading the newspaper and watching the news on television. It is especially important to not listen to negative news before you go to bed. If you fill your mind with the negativity of the day's tragic stories, it will be virtually impossible to follow with positive visualizations of what you want to come into your life. You will be taking one step forward and two steps back. You are sending yourself contradictory information when you listen to tragic stories and then try to focus on the good that is coming to you. Can you see how difficult it is to believe in your forthcoming financial abundance when you hear that the stock market fell one hundred points? If you do read the newspaper, just scan the headlines without reading all of the gory details. I have not read the newspaper, other than the sports section, in eight or ten years and I have not missed it at all. What you really need to know will come to you.

It is equally important to stay away from negative people. There are many people who love to talk about their own misery and the misery of others. They frequently discuss disease, aging, and the failing relationships of their friends and families. When you find yourself in the midst of people who thrive on negativity, it would be in your best interest to excuse yourself or limit the amount of time you spend in their company. If you cannot get away from a discussion that turns negative, simply say to yourself, "That is not my reality" or "That may be your reality, but it is not mine." Limiting your exposure to negativity is a gift you can give yourself, and it will only accelerate your ability to receive divine abundance.

Step 6: Affirm It

Stating that your heart's desires already exist is a pathway to your abundance. Make a commitment to affirm daily what you want to have in your life. As you do so, thank the Universe for meeting your needs in perfect timing. By believing that your needs are already met, you can begin to live a life that is free—free from burdens, frustration, and lack. Confirm your abundance and know that you are taken care of perfectly.

With an open mind and willing heart, bless your own process and have faith that your needs are being met.

This is a very private practice. It isn't that it is a secret, but these are your own individual thoughts and desires. When you discuss your innermost wants and desires with others, their feedback and input can diminish your commitment to change. You can talk your way out of your own good. Do not try to convince others of your new awareness. Everyone has his own path. With an open mind and willing heart, bless your own process and have faith that your needs are being met. Your thoughts, wants, and desires are between you and your Higher Power.

Chapter Twelve Exercises:
What You Can Do

This chapter functions as a sort of guide to help you best attain your heart's desires. Work through the steps as thoroughly and honestly as you can—even if you have trouble believing in the power of this process at first. Think of it this way: you have nothing to lose and everything to gain. Literally. Here are the steps for your review:

- **Step 1:** Write down desires, wants, and goals.
- **Step 2:** Make a "vision board."
- **Step 3:** Visualize it: see it to be it.
- **Step 4:** Prepare to receive your heart's desires by taking action.
- **Step 5:** Abolish doubt.
- **Step 6:** Affirm it.

Thirteen

Mantras and Affirmations

"We can never go back again, that much is certain."
—Daphne du Maurier—

The following is a sampling of mantras and affirmations that will help you practice techniques for living abundantly. Feel free to write your own affirmations or make any changes to the ones below to better fit your wants and desires. Remember to state them in a positive light rather than focusing on what you have that you don't want. When you make a statement regarding what you have but don't want, you are feeding energy into what you do not want and the condition may very well stay with you. The statement "I am" is a simple and effective way to tell the Universe that you believe you deserve abundance.

Remember to take what works for you and leave what doesn't. References to "Divinity," "God," and "the Universe" represent and encompass your personal Higher Power, whatever that may be.

Abundance:

I am now living life abundantly.

I deserve to experience divine abundance because I am a child of God.

Abundance is my birthright. I claim it for myself under grace and in God's perfect timing.

The financial abundance that flows through the Universe is my heritage. It comes to me now.

I believe in the goodness of God. God provides through me in perfect ways.

The Universe is my infinite supply. I am showered with plenty of all that I want and need.

I am gracefully connected to the river of abundance. My supply comes to me in perfect ways and in perfect timing.

I spend money without fear, as I understand that God is my unfailing source.

I release all negative thinking as I claim my inheritance of abundance.

Unlimited abundance comes to me under grace and in perfect ways.

I celebrate God's abundance as I claim it for myself and those whom I love.

Unlimited abundance now comes to me in unlimited ways.

As I enter the promised land with grace, limitation and lack now fall away.

God is my immediate supply. All of my needs are now met in a perfect way.

Infinite Spirit, open the way for my great abundance now. I am an irresistible magnet for all that belongs to me by divine right.

I give thanks that abundance is mine by divine right. It now pours in and piles up, under grace and in perfect ways.

I cast this burden of lack on Christ and I go free to have plenty.

I now thank God, the giver of good, for the gifts I am given.

The unexpected happens. My seemingly impossible good now comes to pass.

From the divine love that flows through my being, I call forth my abundance and prosperity in all forms that will bring me happiness and joy.

Healing:

I am a healthy child of the Universe.

The healing power of God permeates every cell in my body, making my body healthy and whole.

I claim physical healing by releasing any and all thoughts of lack, criticism, and self-pity. I replace negative thinking with thoughts of abundance, blessing, and self-esteem.

My body is the creation of God—whole, healthy, and vibrant.

I deserve to experience optimal health, love, and happiness because I am a child of God.

I see myself as God sees me, filled with energy and vitality.

As I realize my value, I am filled with joy, love, and abundant health.

Divine healing now comes to pass in my body. This is my rightful inheritance.

As I release all resentments, my cells are restored to their natural state of wholeness. I give thanks for my radiant health.

As I release the need to be right, I am restored to wholeness. Serenity is my birthright.

Let me now express the divine idea in my mind, body, and affairs.

I now act with motives of faith and not fear.

Thou in me art:
> eternal joy
> eternal youth
> eternal wealth
> eternal health
> eternal love
> eternal life

Nothing is too good to be true;

Nothing is too wonderful to happen;

Nothing is too good to last.

Relationships:

I am manifesting my healthy relationship.

I give thanks for the divine partner that is coming into my life in God's perfect timing.

I deserve to experience an abundant relationship because I am a child of God.

I was created to be in a joyful relationship. I claim it now as my rightful inheritance.

I love myself. I love others. As a loving being, others love me.

I will attract that which I am. Therefore, as I develop within myself the traits that I deserve and want in a relationship, I will attract that perfect partner.

I am created in the image of God. Because God is love, I am love.

I joyfully wait for the arrival of my divinely chosen partner.

Divine love is maintained in my marriage, through me and for me.

Because I now know my preciousness, I am ready to love and to be loved.

All of my relationships are peaceful and filled with love. I celebrate the magnificence of living life abundantly.

I call forth a sharer, one who is my equal, who will grow as I grow, that we may grow together. So be it.

Protection:

I am protected.

My shield is the love of the Universe. Nothing harmful can penetrate its barrier.

I am safe. God's arms wrap me in protection.

Guidance:

I am now guided.

Divine Intelligence is my partner in every area of my life, and it guides my choices and decisions.

My Higher Power is guiding me down the pathway to abundant life.

God is aligning my will with His will.

My steps are divinely guided, as I trust my intuition.

Happiness:

I am happy.

I celebrate life with joy and wonder because I am a child of the Universe.

Joy is my rightful inheritance! May I experience its fullness and share that joy with others.

I anticipate with joy the experiences that come to me today and every day.

As I express gratitude for _____, joy overflows from my heart.

As I anticipate the goodness of the Universe, I am filled with resounding joy!

God's plan for me is joyful. I am free now to release all fear and negativity.

As you reflect on your specific desires, affirmations will solidify your worthiness. Although you may not receive exactly what you desire, there will be something better. Rejection is God's protection because He wants *only* the best for you.

Unfortunately our timing is not always the timing of the Universe. By being patient and knowing that your heart's desires are already met, you can relax and wait for the abundant flow. Just because you don't feel abundant doesn't mean that your desires are not coming to you. It is easy to second-guess these steps. You may actually find that you try to talk yourself out of them because you have not seen immediate results. Hang in there! Get excited! More will be revealed! You deserve it!

Conclusion

Congratulations! You actually made it all the way through a self-help book. You are beginning to see the world through a different pair of glasses. You have a newfound understanding of shame and the game it has played with your mind, your feelings, and your experiences.

You can see that precious, wounded child inside you that has been ignored for so very long, and you are now embracing him. Even though you may feel anger and sadness about the way that you were treated as a child, you can have some level of compassion for those who did the best they knew how, even if it was not really what you needed.

You can now become a different kind of parent, friend, and partner. You are beginning to actually believe what this book has stressed so adamantly: *you are valuable simply because you exist and you deserve to experience abundance.* Although this is only the beginning of your journey, you will never be able to go back to the place from which you started. Changes have occurred deep within your soul and the effects of these changes will radiate through your being, reaching out to help the world become a better place for all of God's children.

It has been an honor and a privilege to participate in your expedition as you learn to live in the glorious world of self-awareness and self-esteem. I do not claim to know the absolute truth, as that divine knowledge belongs only to the Universe. These are merely my truths, as I know them today. Take what you like and leave the rest. Your Higher Power will reveal your own truth, as you continue to develop as a seeker. Enjoy and relish the seeking. The abundant world is waiting for you!

Words of Wisdom

"For as he thinketh in his heart, so is he."
—Proverbs 23:7—

"Suffering is *always* the effect of wrong
thought in some direction."
—James Allen—

"In the infinity of life, where I am,
All is perfect, whole, and complete.
I am always Divinely protected and guided.
It is safe for me to look within myself.
It is safe for me to look into the past.
It is safe for me to enlarge my viewpoint of life.
I am for more than my personality—
past, present, or future.
I now choose to rise above my personality problems
To recognize the magnificence of my being.
I am totally willing to learn to love myself.
All is well in my world."
—Louise Hay—

"She lacks confidence, she craves admiration insatiably. She
lives on the reflections of herself in the eyes of others. She
does not dare to be herself."
—Anaïs Nin—

"A complete revolution takes place in your physical and mental
being when you've laughed and had some fun."
—Catherine Ponder—

"Within our dreams and aspirations we find our opportunities."
—Sue Atchley Ebaugh

"I want to get you excited about who
you are, what you are, what you have, and what can
still be for you. I want to inspire you to see that you
can go far beyond where you are right now."
—Virginia Satir—

"Love is an expression and assertion of self-esteem,
a response to one's own values in the person of another."
—Ayn Rand—

"Those who do not know how to weep
with their whole hearts don't know how to laugh either."
—Golda Meir—

"Change occurs when one becomes what she is, not
when she tries to become what she is not."
—Ruth P. Freedman—

"You grow up the day you have the first real laugh at yourself."
—Ethel Barrymore—

"There is a price which is too great to pay
for peace, and that price can be put in one word.
One cannot pay the price of self-respect."
—Woodrow Wilson—

". . . Human beings, by changing the inner attitudes of their
minds, can change the outer aspects of their lives."
—William James—

"Our very life depends on everything's
Recurring till we answer from within."
—Robert Frost—

"The battle to keep up appearances
unnecessarily, the mask—whatever name you give creeping
perfectionism—robs us of our energies."
—Robin Worthington—

"Follow your dream. Take one step at a time and don't settle
for less, just continue to climb."
—Amanda Bradley—

"From early infancy onward we all incorporate into our lives
the message we receive concerning our self-worth, or lack of
self-worth, and this sense of value is to be found beneath our
actions and feelings as a tangled network of self-perception."
—Christina Baldwin—

"One receives only that which is given. The game of life is a
game of boomerangs. Our thoughts, deeds and words return
to us sooner or later with astounding accuracy."
—Florence Scovel Shinn—

"The Universe is run exactly on the lines
of a cafeteria. Unless you claim—mentally—what
you want, you may sit and wait forever."
—Emmet Fox—

"A tragic mistake that is often made is to assume that the will of God is bound to be something very dull and uninviting, if not positively unpleasant . . . The truth is that the will of God for us always means greater freedom, greater self-expression, newer and brighter experience, wider opportunity for service to others—life more abundant."
—Emmet Fox—

"How I relate to my inner self influences my relationships with all others. My satisfaction with myself and my satisfaction with other people are directly proportional."
—Sue Atchley Ebaugh—

"The journey of a thousand miles begins with a single step."
—Lao-tzu—

"Your vision will become clear only when you can look into your own heart."
—Carl Jung—

"The past has flown away,
The coming month and year do not exist;
Ours only is the present's tiny point."
—Mahmud Shabistari—

"If a man carries his own lantern, he need not fear darkness."
—Hasidic saying—

"In the midst of winter, I finally learned that there was in me an invincible summer."
—Albert Camus—

"Fear is only an illusion. It is the illusion that
creates the feeling of separateness—the false sense of
isolation that exists only in your imagination."
—Jeraldine Saunders—

"She had trouble defining herself independently of her
husband, tried to talk to him about it, but he said nonsense,
he had no trouble defining her at all."
—Cynthia Propper Seton—

"As I walk, As I walk,
The Universe is walking with me."
—From the Navajo rain dance ceremony—

"For here we are not afraid to follow
truth wherever it may lead . . . "
—Thomas Jefferson—

"Years may wrinkle the skin, but to give
up enthusiasm wrinkles the soul."
—Samuel Ullman—

"I look in the mirror through the eyes of
the child that was me."
—Judy Collins—

"We have seen too much defeatism, too much pessimism,
too much of a negative approach. The answer is simple: if
you want something very badly, you can achieve it. It may take
patience, very hard work, a real struggle, and a long time, but it
can be done . . . faith is a prerequisite of any undertaking."
—Margo Jones—

"If we do not change our direction,
we are likely to end up where we are headed."
—Chinese proverb—

"This above all: to thine own self be true."
—William Shakespeare—

"We should have much peace if we would not busy ourselves
with the sayings and doings of others."
—Thomas à Kempis—

"There is a guidance for each of us, and by lowly
listening we shall hear the right word . . . Place yourself in
the middle of the stream of power and wisdom which
flows into your life. Then, without effort, you are impelled
to truth and to perfect contentment."
—Ralph Waldo Emerson—

"To love oneself is the beginning of a lifelong romance."
—Oscar Wilde—

"Do what you can, with what you have, where you are."
—Theodore Roosevelt—

"It is the chiefest point of happiness that a man is willing to be
what he is."
—Desiderius Erasmus—

"We are what we repeatedly do. Excellence,
then, is not an act, but a habit."
—Aristotle—

"Let one therefore keep the mind pure, for what
a man thinks that he becomes . . ."
—The Upanishads—

"My imperfections and failures are as much a
blessing from God as my successes and my talents,
and I lay them both at His feet."
—Mahatma Gandhi—

"The ultimate lesson all of us have to learn is unconditional
love, which includes not only others but ourselves as well."
—Elisabeth Kübler-Ross—

"If one advances confidently in the direction of his dreams,
and endeavors to live the life which he has imagined, he will
meet with a success unexpected in common hours."
—Henry David Thoreau—

". . . sometimes it is necessary to reteach a thing its loveliness . . .
until it flowers again from within . . ."
—Galway Kinnell—

"It is difficult to make a man miserable while
he feels worthy of himself and claims kindred to the
great God who made him."
—Abraham Lincoln—

"The intellect has little to do on the road to
discovery. There comes a leap in consciousness, call it intuition
or what you will, the solution comes to you and
you don't know how or why."
—Albert Einstein—

"The past is but the beginning of a beginning . . ."
—H.G. Wells—

"You get to the point where your demons, which are terrifying,
get smaller and smaller and you get bigger and bigger."
—August Wilson—

"Life holds so much—so much to be so happy about always.
Most people ask for happiness on conditions. Happiness can
be felt only if you don't set conditions."
—Arthur Rubinstein—

"If a man happens to find himself, he has a mansion which he
can inhabit with dignity all the days of his life."
—James A. Michener—

"Anything forced into manifestation through personal will is
always 'ill got' and has 'ever bad success.'"
—Florence Scovel Shinn—

"Tears are like rain. They loosen up our soil
so we can grow in different directions."
—Virginia Casey—

"Desire and longing are the whips of God."
—Anna Wickham—

"There is a Divine plan of good at work in my life.
I will let go and let it unfold."
—Ruth P. Freedman—

"I exist as I am—that is enough;
If no other in the world be aware, I sit content;
And if each and all be aware, I sit content."
—Walt Whitman—

"Be not afraid of growing slowly.
Be afraid only of standing still."
—Chinese proverb—

"Change your thoughts and you change your world."
—Norman Vincent Peale—

"Each indecision brings its own delays and days are lost
lamenting over lost days. . . . What you can do or think you can
do, begin it. For boldness has magic, power, and genius in it."
—Johann Wolfgang von Goethe—

"Be still and know that I am with you."
—English prayer—

"He that respects himself is safe from others;
he wears a coat of mail that none can pierce."
—Henry Wadsworth Longfellow—

"Resolve to be thyself; and know,
that he who finds himself, loses his misery."
—Matthew Arnold—

"And the world cannot be discovered by a journey of
miles . . . but only by a spiritual journey . . . by which we arrive
at the ground at our feet, and learn to be at home."
—Wendell Berry—

For those who were raised in a religious environment, the following biblical scriptures can be useful as you come to believe that you deserve abundance:

"Ask, and it shall be given you; seek, and ye shall find; knock, and it shall be opened unto you."
—Matthew 7:7—

"The eternal God is thy refuge, and underneath are the everlasting arms . . ."
—Deuteronomy 33:27—

"According to your faith be it unto you."
—Matthew 9:29—

"For with God all things are possible."
—Mark 10:27—

"For God giveth to a man that is good in his sight wisdom, and knowledge, and joy . . ."
—Ecclesiastes 2:26—

"Not rendering evil for evil, or railing for railing; but contrariwise blessing; knowing that ye are thereunto called, that ye should inherit a blessing."
—1 Peter 3:9—

"If ye then, being evil, know how to give good gifts unto your children, how much more shall your Father which is in heaven give good things to them that ask him?"
—Matthew 7:11—

"So God created man in his own image,
in the image of God created he him . . ."
—Genesis 1:27—

"But my God shall supply all your need according
to his riches in glory by Christ Jesus."
—Philippians 4:19—

"Cast thy burden upon the Lord, and he shall sustain thee . . ."
—Psalm 55:22—

"The Lord is able to give thee much more than this."
—2 Chronicles 25:9—

"For I am the Lord that healeth thee."
—Exodus 15:26—

"If ye shall ask any thing in my name, I will do it."
—John 14:14—

". . . I am come that they might have life, and
that they might have it more abundantly."
—John 10:10—

"Let not your heart be troubled, neither let it be afraid."
—John 14:27—

"For my yoke is easy, and my burden is light."
—Matthew 11:30—

"Behold, I make all things new."
—Revelation 21:5—

"For this God is our God for ever and ever:
he will be our guide even unto death."
—Psalm 48:14—

"Ho, everyone that thirsteth, come ye to the waters, and he that
hath no money; come ye, buy, and eat . . ."
—Isaiah 55:1—

"And this commandment have we from him, That he who
loveth God love his brother also."
—1 John 4:21—

"Finally, brethren, whatsoever things are true,
whatsoever things are honest, whatsoever things are just,
whatsoever things are pure, whatsoever things are lovely,
whatsoever things are of good report; if there be any virtue,
and if there be any praise, think on these things."
—Philippians 4:8—

". . . pray to thy Father which is in secret; and thy Father which
seeth in secret shall reward thee openly."
—Matthew 6:6—

"Wherefore, if God so clothe the grass of the field . . . shall he
not much more clothe you, O ye of little faith?"
—Matthew 6:30—

"Take therefore no thought for the morrow: for the morrow
shall take thought for the things of itself."
—Matthew 6:34—

"For the word of God is quick and powerful . . ."
—Hebrews 4:12—

"And let us not be weary in well doing:
for in due season we shall reap, if we faint not."
—Galatians 6:9—

"Delight thyself also in the Lord: and
he shall give thee the desires of thine heart."
—Psalm 37:4—

"And being fully persuaded that, what he had
promised, he was able also to perform."
—Romans 4:21—

". . . and all of you are children of the most High."
—Psalm 82:6—

"God is love; and he that dwelleth in
love dwelleth in God, and God in him."
—1 John 4:16—

Recommended Reading

I want to express a great deal of gratitude for the following books and highly recommend them to my readers.

Abundance:

Beattie, Melody. *Choices*. San Francisco: HarperSanFrancisco, 2002.

———. *The Lessons of Love*. San Francisco: HarperSanFrancisco, 1994.

Beck, Charlotte Joko. *Everyday Zen*. San Francisco: Harper & Row, 1989.

Byrne, Rhonda. *The Secret*. Hillsboro, OR: Beyond Words Publishing, 2006.

The Dalai Lama and Howard C. Cutler. *The Art of Happiness*. New York: Riverhead Books, 1998.

Dyer, Wayne W. *Manifest Your Destiny*. New York: HarperCollins, 1997.

———. *Your Sacred Self*. New York: HarperCollins, 1995.

Fox, Emmet. *Alter Your Life*. San Francisco: HarperSanFrancisco, 1994.

————. *Diagrams for Living*. San Francisco: HarperSanFrancisco, 1993.

————. *The Sermon on the Mount*. San Francisco: Harper & Row, 1989.

Gattuso, Joan M. *A Course in Love*. San Francisco: HarperSanFranciso, 1996.

Kasl, Charlotte. *If the Buddha Dated*. New York: Penguin/ Arkana, 1999.

————. *If the Buddha Married*. New York: Penguin Compass, 2001.

Losier, Michael, J. *Law of Attraction*. New York: Wellness Central, 2007.

Ponder, Catherine. *Dare to Prosper*. Marina del Rey, CA: DeVorss, 1983.

————. *The Dynamic Laws of Prosperity*. Englewood Cliffs, NJ: Prentice-Hall, 1962.

————. *The Prosperity Secret of the Ages*. Englewood Cliffs, NJ: Prentice-Hall, 1964.

Real, Terrence. *How Can I Get Through to You?* New York: Scribner, 2002.

Real, Terrance. *The New Rules of Marriage*. New York: Ballantine Books, 2007.

Ruiz, Miguel. *The Mastery of Love*. San Rafael, CA: Amber-Allen Publishing, 1999.

Shinn, Florence Scovel. *The Collected Writings of Florence Scovel Shinn*. Radford, VA: Wilder Publications, 2008.

Williamson, Marianne. *A Return to Love*. New York: HarperCollins, 1992.

————. *Enchanted Love*. New York: Simon & Schuster, 1999.

Healing The Wounded Child:

Adams, Kenneth M. *Silently Seduced*. Deerfield Beach, FL: Health Communications, 1991.

Beattie, Melody. *Codependent No More*. Center City, MN: Hazelden, 1987.

Bradshaw, John. *Healing the Shame that Binds You*. Deerfield Beach, FL.; Health Communications, 2005.

Downs, Alan. *The Velvet Rage: Overcoming the Pain of Growing Up Gay in a Straight Man's World*. Cambridge, MA: De Capo Lifelong, 2005.

Forward, Susan. *Toxic Parents*. New York: Bantam Books, 1989.

Gil, Eliana. *Outgrowing the Pain*. San Franciso: Launch Press, 1983.

Hay, Louise. *You Can Heal Your Life*. Santa Monica, CA: Hay House, 1987.

Herman, Judith, MD. *Trauma and Recovery*. New York: BasicBooks, 1997.

Jeffers, Susan, MD. *Feel the Fear and Do It Anyway*. New York: Fawcett Columbine Books.

Katherine, Anne. *Boundaries: Where You End and I Begin*. New York: Fireside, 1993.

Lerner, Harriet, PhD. *The Dance of Anger*. New York: Harper & Row, 1985.

———. *The Dance of Intimacy*. New York: Harper & Row, 1989.

Mellody, Pia, Andrea Wells Miller, and J. Keith Miller. *Facing Codependence*. San Francisco: Perennial Library, 1989.

———. *Facing Love Addiction*. New York: HarperSanFrancisco, 1992.

Mellody, Pia and Lawrence S. Freundlich. *The Intimacy Factor.* San Francisco: HarperSanFrancisco, 2003.

Miller, Alice. *The Drama of the Gifted Child.* New York: Basic Books, 1997.

Real, Terrence. *I Don't Want to Talk About It.* New York: Fireside, 1998.

Wortitz, Janet Geringer. *Adult Children of Alcoholics.* Pompano Beach, FL: Health Communications, 1987.

————. *Struggle for Intimacy.* Pompano Beach, FL: Health Communications, 1985.

Spirituality:

Allen, James. *As a Man Thinketh.* Thomas Y. Crowell, 1913.

Barks, Coleman, trans. *The Essential Rumi.* San Francisco: Harper, 1995.

The Bible.

Chopra, Deepak. *Buddha.* New York: HarperSanFrancisco, 2007.

————. *The Seven Spiritual Laws of Success.* San Rafael, CA: Amber-Allen Publishing, 1994.

Kurtz, Ernest, and Katherine Ketcham. *The Spirituality of Imperfection.* New York: Bantam Books, 1992.

Frankl, Viktor E. *A Man's Search for Meaning.* New York: Pocket Books, 1985.

Foundation for Inner Peace. *A Course in Miracles: Combined Volume.* Glen Elen, CA: Foundation for Inner Peace, 1992.

Hagen, Steve. *Buddhism Plain and Simple.* New York: Broadway Books, 1999.

Kornfield, Jack. *A Path with Heart.* New York: Bantam Books, 1993.

Merton, Thomas. *Thoughts in Solitude.* New York: Noonday Press.

Nouwen, Henri J.M. *Life of the Beloved.* New York: Crossroad Publishing, 1992.

Peck, M. Scott, M.D. *The Road Less Traveled.* New York: Simon and Schuster, 1978.

Prince, Joseph. *Destined to Reign Devotional.* Tulsa, OK: Harrison House, 2008.

Smedes, Lewis B. *Shame and Grace.* San Francisco: HarperSanFrancisco, 1993.

Tolle, Eckhart. *A New Earth: Awakening to Your Life's Purpose.* New York: Dutton/Penguin Group, 2005.

―――. *The Power of Now.* Novato, CA: New World Library, 1999.

Torkington, David. *The Hermit.* New York: Alba House, 1977.

―――. *The Mystic.* New York: Alba House, 1995.

―――. *The Prophet.* New York: Alba House, 1987.

Trungpa, Chögyam. *Meditation in Action.* Boston: Shambhala Publications, 1991.

Watts, Alan W. *The Wisdom of Insecurity.* New York: Pantheon, 1951.

About the Author

photo by
Rusty Bradford Photography

Janice Sterling Gaunt, LPC, graduated with a bachelor's degree from Texas Tech University and a master of arts degree from Amberton University. She has trained extensively with Terrence Real, founder of the Relational Life Institute, and Pia Mellody, senior clinical advisor for The Meadows. Janice is a practicing counselor specializing in helping both individuals and couples experience abundant living as they overcome the effects of their own childhood trauma. Janice is available for private sessions, public speaking, and workshops. She lives with her husband in Dallas.

For more information about Janice or *The Shame Game*, please visit janicegaunt.com.